ABANDONED CHICAGOLAND

RUST ON THE PRAIRIES

JERRY OLEJNICZAK

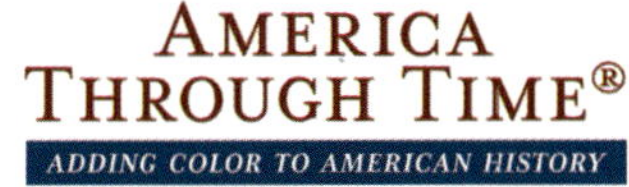

America Through Time is an imprint of Fonthill Media LLC
www.through-time.com
office@through-time.com

Published by Arcadia Publishing by arrangement with Fonthill Media LLC
For all general information, please contact Arcadia Publishing:
Telephone: 843-853-2070
Fax: 843-853-0044
E-mail: sales@arcadiapublishing.com
For customer service and orders:
Toll-Free 1-888-313-2665

www.arcadiapublishing.com

First published 2021

ISBN 978-1-63499-329-6

Typeset in Trade Gothic
Printed and bound in England

CONTENTS

ABOUT THE AUTHOR

JERRY OLEJNICZAK has been awed by places abandoned, forgotten, or otherwise on the sidelines of society since he was a kid. On trips to his family's native Poland, he would thrill at the post-WWII ruins or empty construction sites he could visit in the then Eastern-Bloc country. As an adult, he began to cautiously try his hand at exploring the abandoned buildings he would pass occasionally at work. Soon, he bought a camera to document the unique beauty of the places he was finding.

Jerry has lived most of his life in or around Chicago. He currently resides in Oak Park, Illinois, with his wife and two cats. You can find more of his work at his blog, Tabularasaphoto.org.

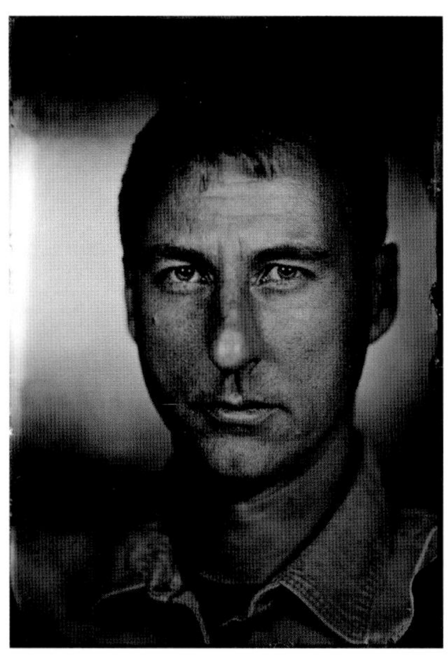

INTRODUCTION

Chicago is a world class metropolis, with cultural and historic significance greater than merely being the largest city between the American coasts or the economic engine of the Midwest. Mention Chicago anywhere around the world, and you're likely to get at least a glimmer of recognition. That may often take the form of finger guns accompanied by "rat-a-tat" noises, a nod to Al Capone. Sports fans associate the city with Michael Jordan and his dominance of professional basketball in the nineties. Chicago is also renowned for its architecture, being the birthplace of the skyscraper, as well as where improv comedy was first performed. It is a vibrant city, one that seemingly escaped the mid-century upheaval of urban decay and depopulation that affected so many other Midwestern towns. But the key word here is "seemingly." The dynamics that turned much of the Rust Belt into ruins happened here, too, albeit less severely and in more nuanced ways. Businesses didn't flee the city center; rather, the slide into urban decay happened on the peripheries, in outlying areas and suburbs, where it could be more easily overlooked. The south side of the city, historically home to most of its African-American population as well as many immigrants, boasted the busiest stockyards in the world, earning the city the nickname "hog butcher to the world." Along the southern lakefront, huge steel mills dotted the shore. Only about 10 miles south, the town of Gary, Indiana, was gutted when many of its steel mills shuttered or downsized, leaving behind a ruined and impoverished town as the majority of its white residents fled after the 1960s. These events, happening far from the downtown center of the Loop and to less politically empowered people, loom dimly today in our collective consciousness. Chicagoans may think of their city as a patchwork quilt of ethnic neighborhoods, or a burgeoning business and shopping center, but it remains, fundamentally, a blue-collar Rust Belt town made good.

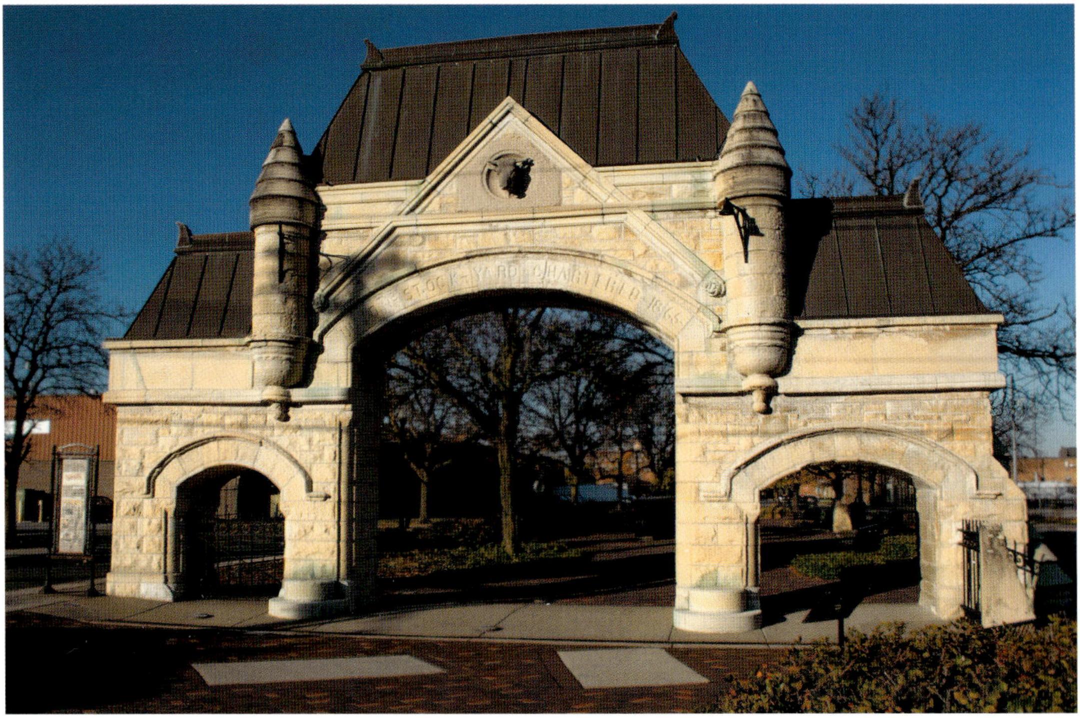

The main gate is the only thing left of the defunct Union Stock Yards.

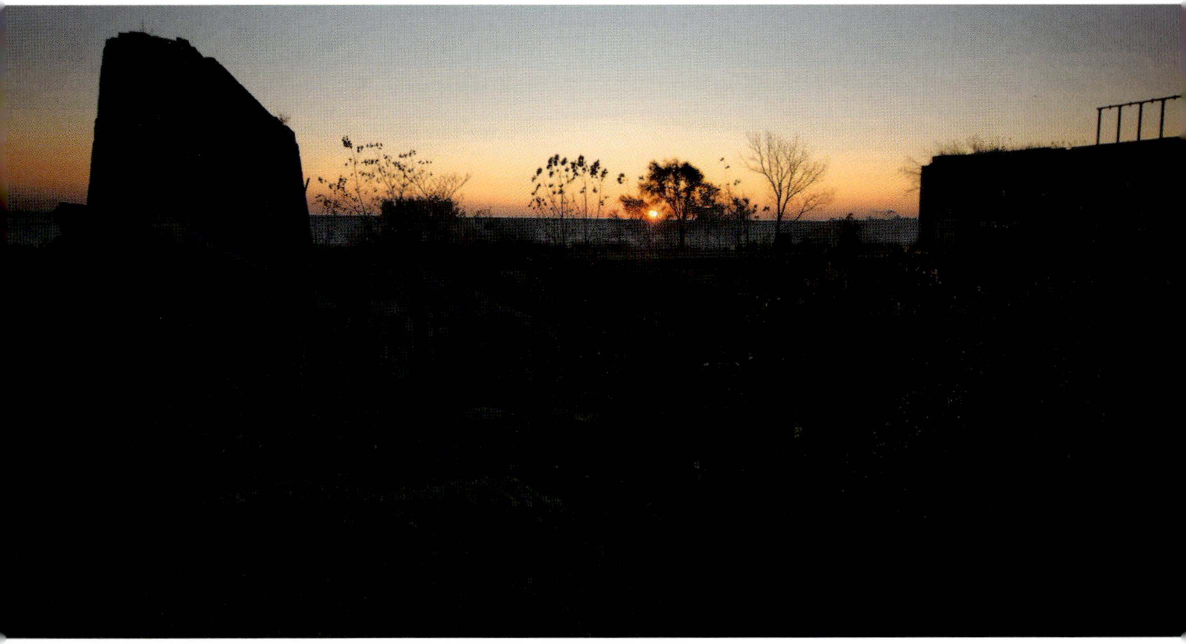

Sun rises over the old U.S. Steel plant.

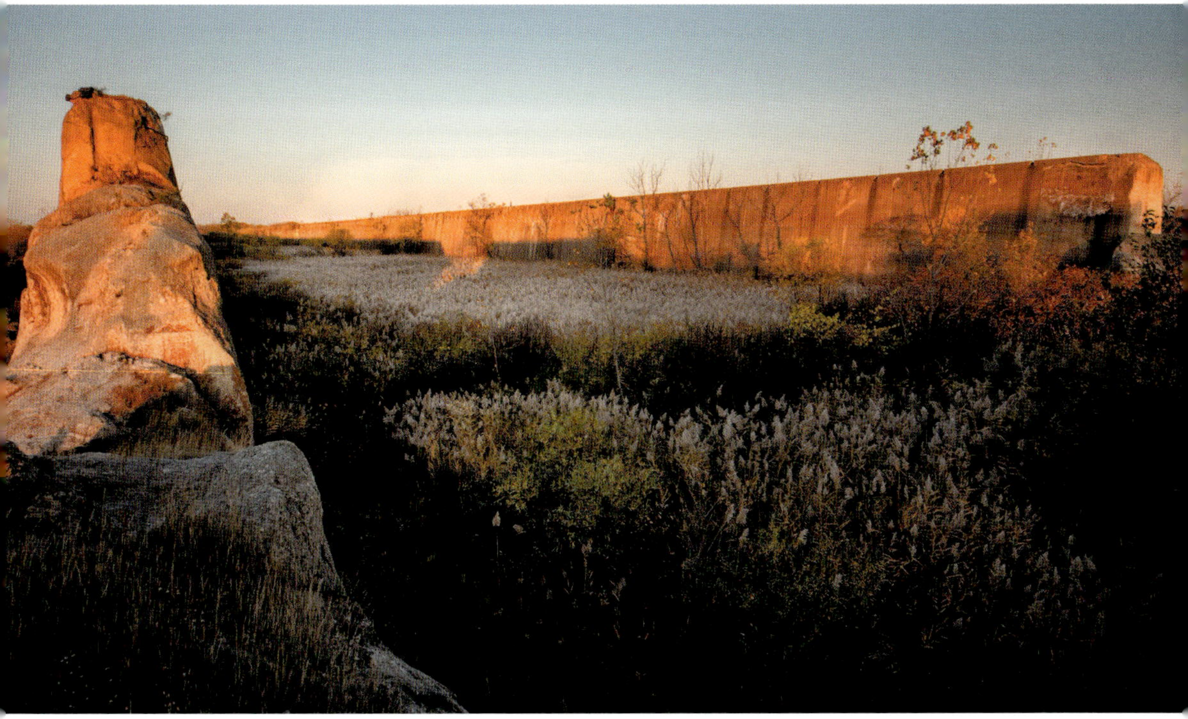

Prairie reclaims land between the old ore walls.

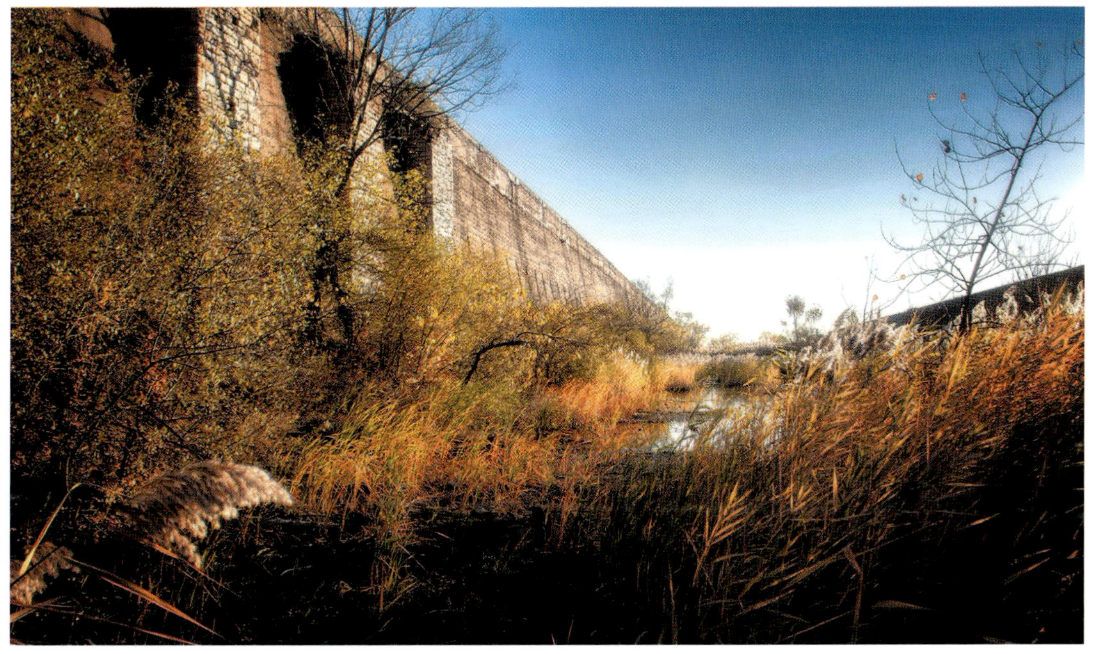

The massive ore walls in places resemble medieval fortifications.

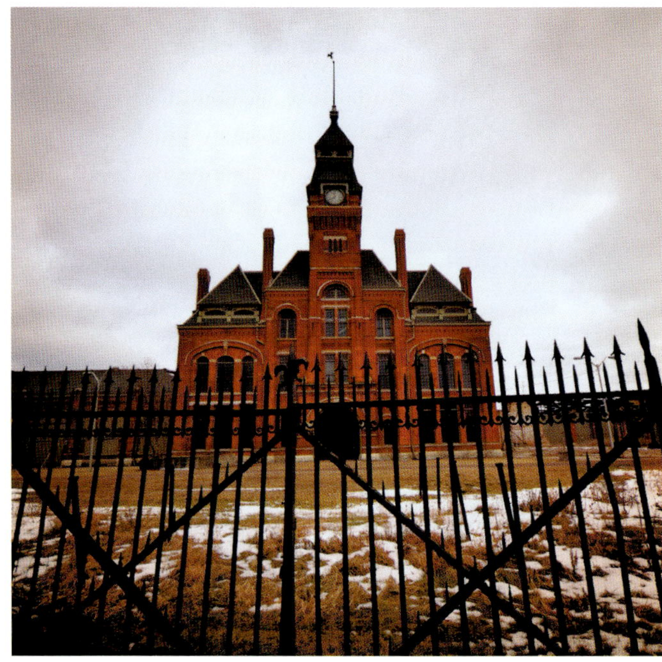

The former headquarters of the Pullman sleeper car company.

If one knows where to look, the vestiges of that iron and concrete city can still be found. Today's glittering skyline and sterile yuppie neighborhoods belie the fact that this city was the setting of Upton Sinclair's *The Jungle* and Lorraine Hansberry's *A Raisin in the Sun*, an urban expanse of tenements, smokestacks, soot, and grime. The photographs in this book hope to capture some of that older city, one that hearkens back to the image painted by Carl Sandburg over a century ago in his poem, "Chicago":

> Fierce as a dog with tongue lapping for action, cunning as a savage pitted against the wilderness,
> Bareheaded,
> Shoveling,
> Wrecking,
> Planning,
> Building, breaking, rebuilding,
> Under the smoke, dust all over his mouth, laughing with white teeth,
> Under the terrible burden of destiny laughing as a young man laughs,
> Laughing even as an ignorant fighter laughs who has never lost a battle,
> Bragging and laughing that under his wrist is the pulse, and under his ribs the heart of the people,
> Laughing!
> Laughing the stormy, husky, brawling laughter of Youth, half-naked, sweating, proud to be Hog Butcher, Tool Maker, Stacker of Wheat, Player with Railroads and Freight Handler to the Nation.

1

URBAN EXPLORATION

Urban exploration (or urbex for short) has become well known, even trendy, in recent years. The term is a rather vague one, used to describe many related activities and the motivations behind them. The modern notoriety of the movement can be traced to photographers such as Camilo Jose Vergara and Richard Nickel, each of whom used their work to raise awareness around a particular issue. Vergara offered a conversation about how and why urban areas change; he once advocated for central Detroit to be set aside as a ruins park, something he dubbed an "American acropolis." Nickel photographed in Chicago at a time when the city's esteem of its architectural heritage was at its nadir; he used his photographs to highlight buildings being torn down and advocated passionately for their conservation. Conversely, many explorers today photograph essentially only to prove they, in fact, have gained access to a particular building or place. Others, stung by criticism in media of urbex photography as "ruinporn," seek to burnish what they do by hearkening back to Nickel and accompanying their photos with histories and calls for conservation.

Often, exploring a particular site may entail dangers, either physical or legal. Thankfully, few explore sheerly to document their daredevilry. Nonetheless, it is true that not many get into this genre of photography purely for love of history or conservation, either. And some would suggest not every old church and factory is historically significant and needs to be saved or preserved. As cities change, technology advances, or populations shift, buildings may become obsolete. They may be too expensive to rehab—or the edifice itself becomes too aged and decayed to salvage.

Ancient Romans called a spirit living in a particular place its *genius loci*. The term today is used to describe the very essence of a location; the emotion and memory evoked simply by being there. This sense of place can be very strong in old and derelict buildings, often as much or more so than when they were in use. It can be in the stunning drama of the decay itself, the timelessness of the architecture, or the pathos of objects left behind. It can also be the preternatural stillness and calm that can be found amidst the noise and bustle of a busy city, if one just slips through the right door or window. Humans are drawn to drama and mystery, and in the abandoned halls of crumbling buildings, both qualities can be found by those intrepid enough to seek them out. This is the motivation, I believe, that drives most urban explorers.

Thus, when urbex photography is labelled as ruinporn, it stings because it's not entirely an unfounded slur. But just as there is pornography, there can also be erotica, with overlap between the two. This type of photography can on one end be entirely genre bound, reaching for the basest pathos, or it can strive to capture the unique beauty that can only be found in man-made structures left to nature. It can be base and maudlin, with its tropes and staged props, or it can reach for something deeper. So, just as pornography and erotica both titillate, but only the latter can be called "art," a similar distinction can hopefully be made between ruinporn and urbex photography. Both tacitly celebrate the processes of decay and abandonment, but the best of the genre can truly convey the sensation of being present in these forgotten places, their *genius loci.*

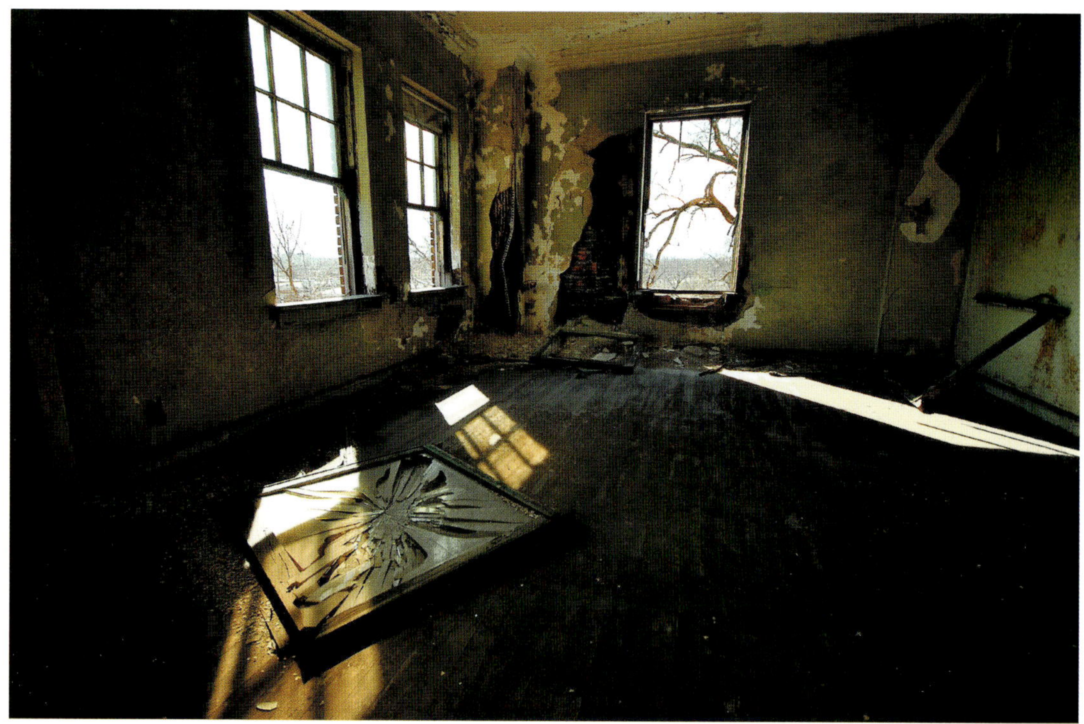

The now demolished Ambassador Apartments were a seven-story urbex playground.

2

APPROACH

Some places visited by urbexers are off the beaten path; others can be hiding in plain sight. Finding them can be an ordeal in itself, involving aimless driving around or scouring Google satellite images for promising leads. Often, like-minded friends online will share or trade info on locations and the challenges involved in accessing them. It's a fraught process, as many explorers are understandably protective of their finds, worried that too many people coming through will attract more security or the wrong kind of visitors, ones eager to trash the place. There is a curious double standard in the urbex community which implicitly lauds the decay, age, and vandalism that might make a place worthy of visiting and photographing in the first place but condemns it as it continues on until its end in utter ruin or demolition. But it is a brand of protectionism that is perhaps necessary, when visiting these sites can range from merely unsafe to entirely illegal.

Still, trespassing or breaking in isn't always necessary. Some finds are standing right in the open, if one knows where to find them. This particular area on Chicago's south side is not entirely abandoned; but when a new bridge was constructed over a river, the old one was left standing right next to it.

The surrounding marshland is striking, as so much unused land well within the city limits is unusual and makes for a distinct framing.

In the suburb of Harvey stands this medieval looking structure. Its appearance and condition has led to it being branded "Bum's Castle," but scant information can be found about what purpose it once served. The most likely theory was that it was meant to be a grain silo, but encroaching urbanization into what had previously been farmland led to it being unfinished and abandoned. Whatever the case may be, the result is a structure that would look more at home on the shores of a Scottish loch than a Midwestern rail line.

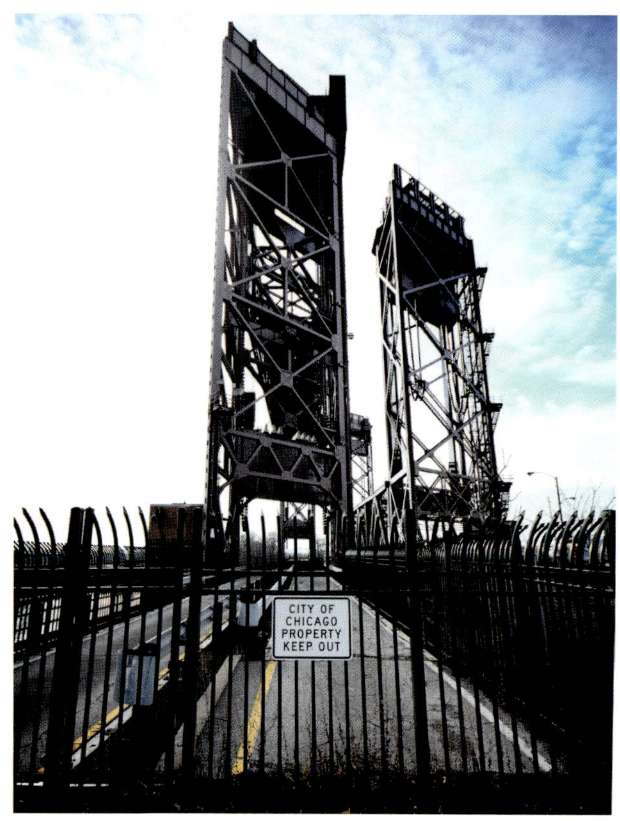

Left: Torrence Avenue bridge stands over the Calumet River.

Below: The bridge as viewed with dumped car in foreground.

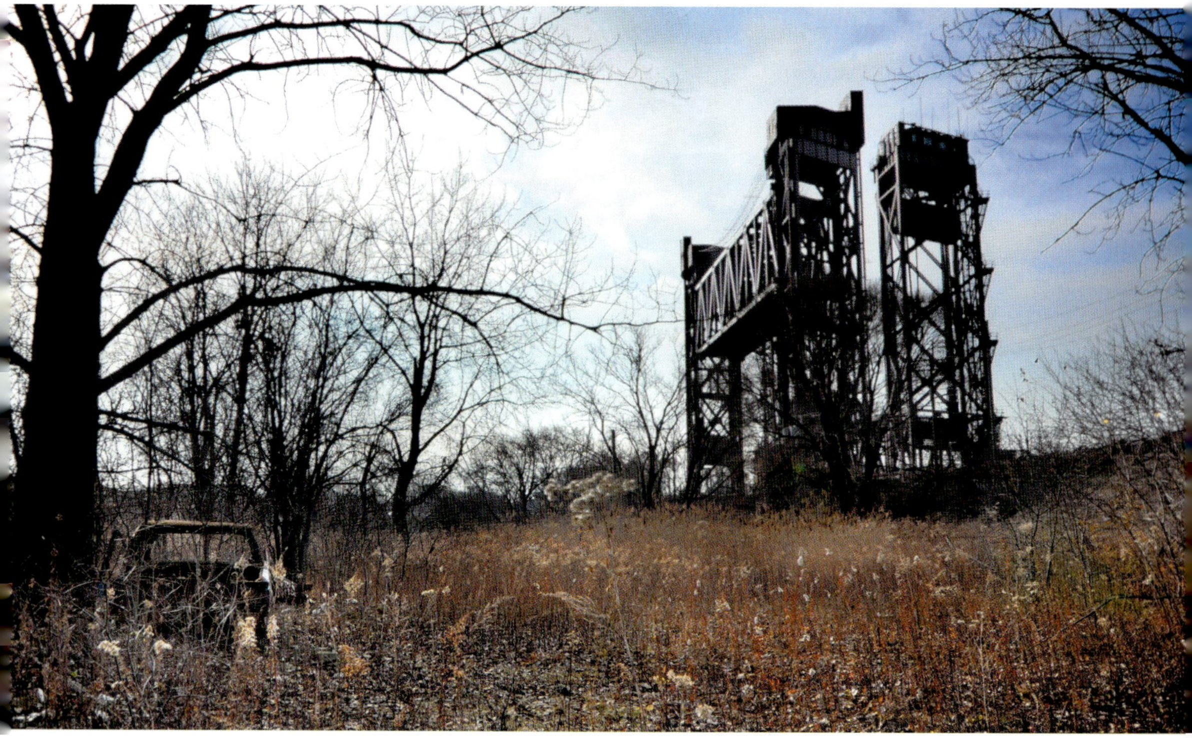

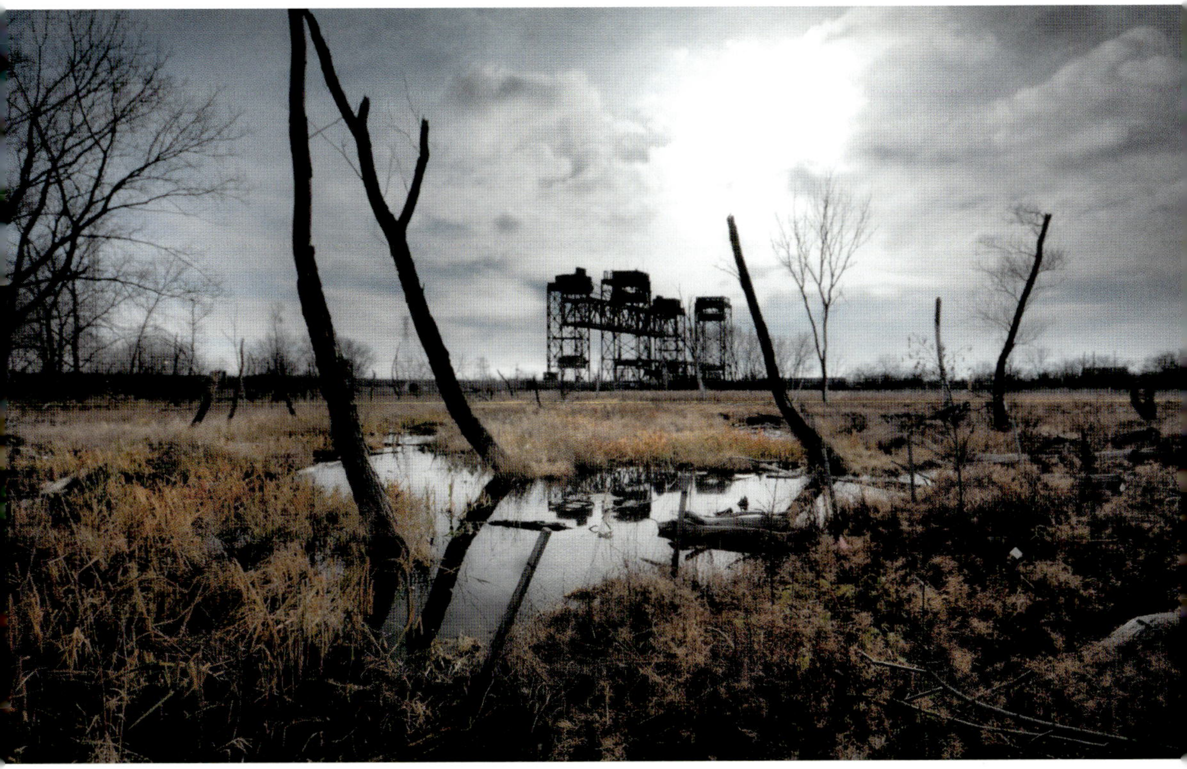

Real American prairie can be found in many places within the city limits of Chicago.

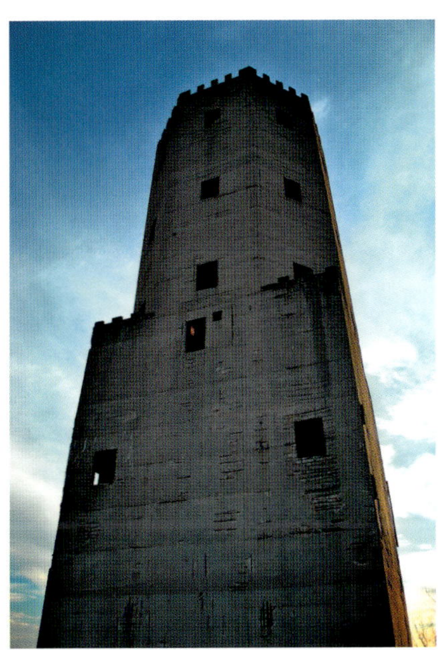

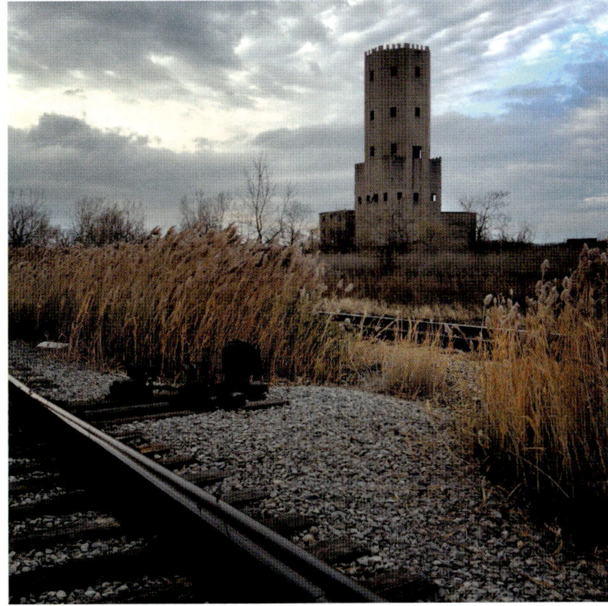

Above left: Hobo Tower is a visual landmark in Harvey, Illinois.

Above right: The tower looms over the adjacent tracks.

Elsewhere on the south side, an urban prairie opens amidst the acres of heavy industry and miles of railroad tracks. A cautious approach leads one through a dense field of tall grasses, which finally begin to thin and yield a view of the coke plant which once stood there. Though most of this campus was razed, a few outbuildings still stand along the peripheries. However, at its core are the twin smokestacks, perhaps too cumbersome or expensive to have been torn down. Their position on this vast field only serves to dramatize their height.

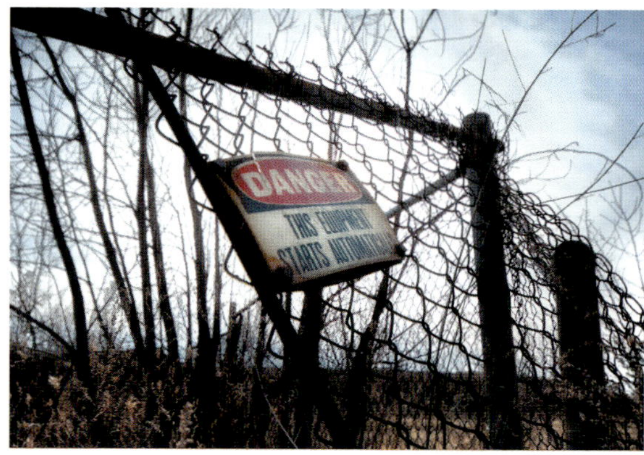

Left: Fear not, kind reader. Upon coming to this sign, I tread no further.

Below: An old coke plant sprouts from the grasses.

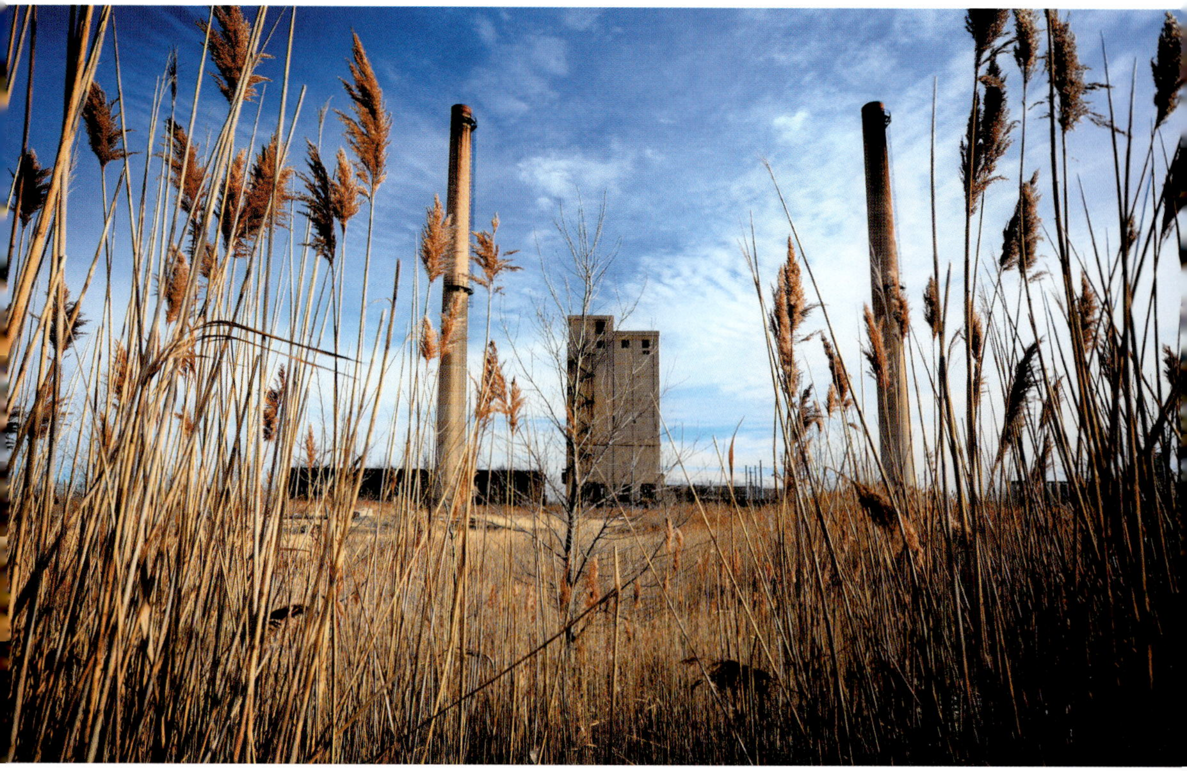

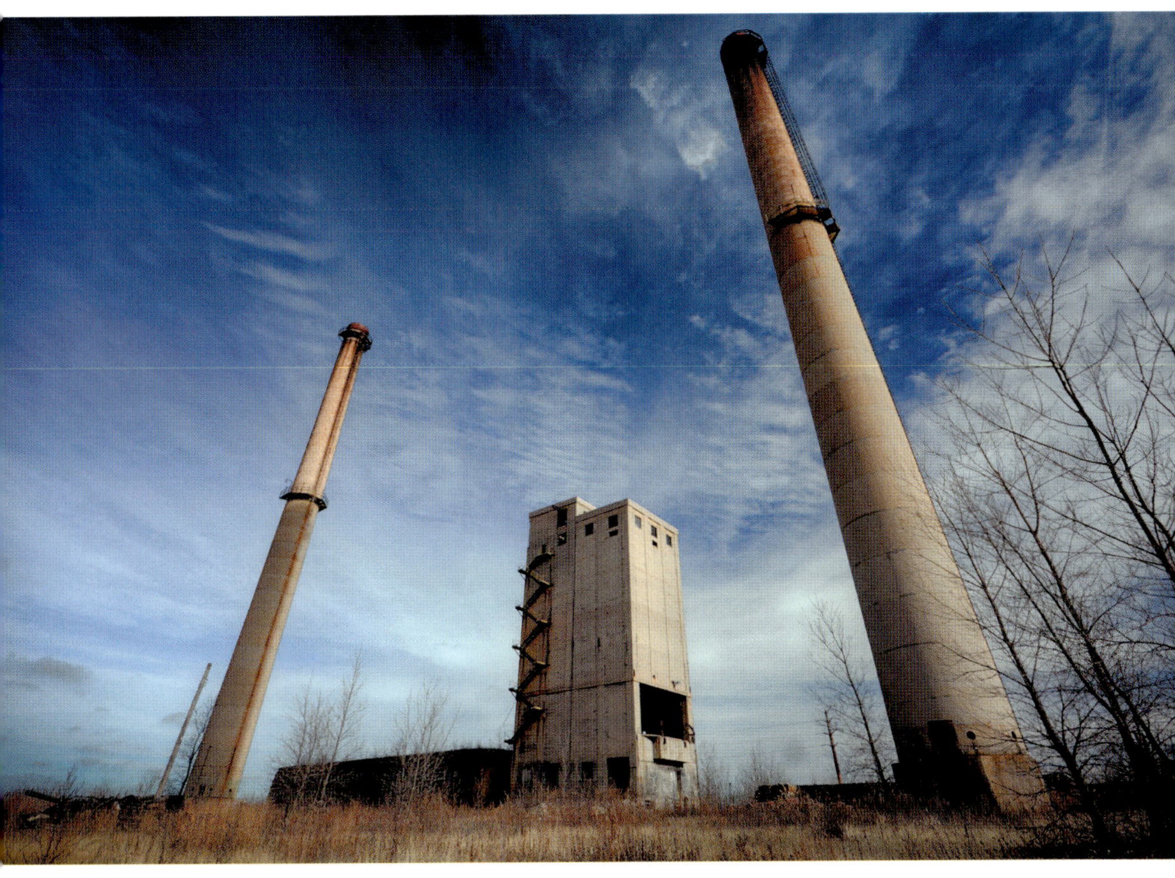

This is most of what remains of Acme Coke.

One of the advantages of finding abandoned places outdoors is you get to see them change with the seasons. This athletic complex of a shuttered high school included, among other things, a football stadium and tennis courts. I first came across these in January, with a damp fog blanketing the area and all the colors muted by winter's cold.

A return in the summer did not disappoint. The tennis courts were barely visible from the road, drowning as they were in dense, lush foliage. The setting sun lit up the leaves and made them glow with its warm light.

Similarly, under winter's dull skies, the stadium was a grim edifice of steel and graffiti. Summertime would revive the bushes and trees at the base of the bleachers, and these would seem to storm up the stands, their leaves whipped by winds.

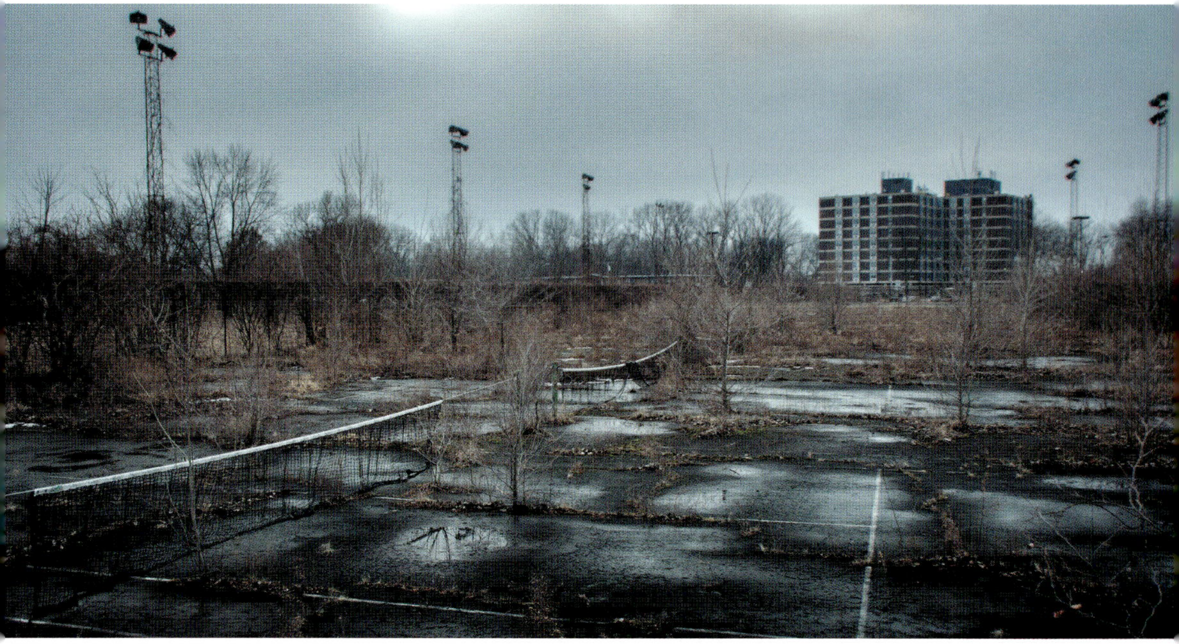

Nature is reclaiming these Gary tennis courts.

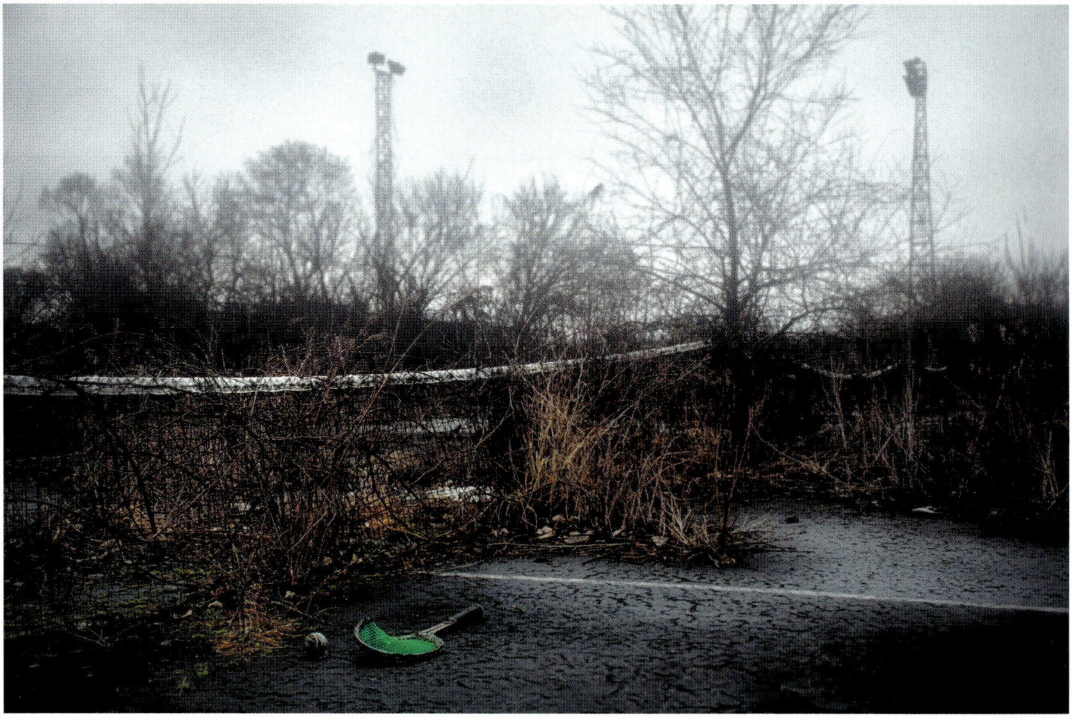

A racket lies in the January fog.

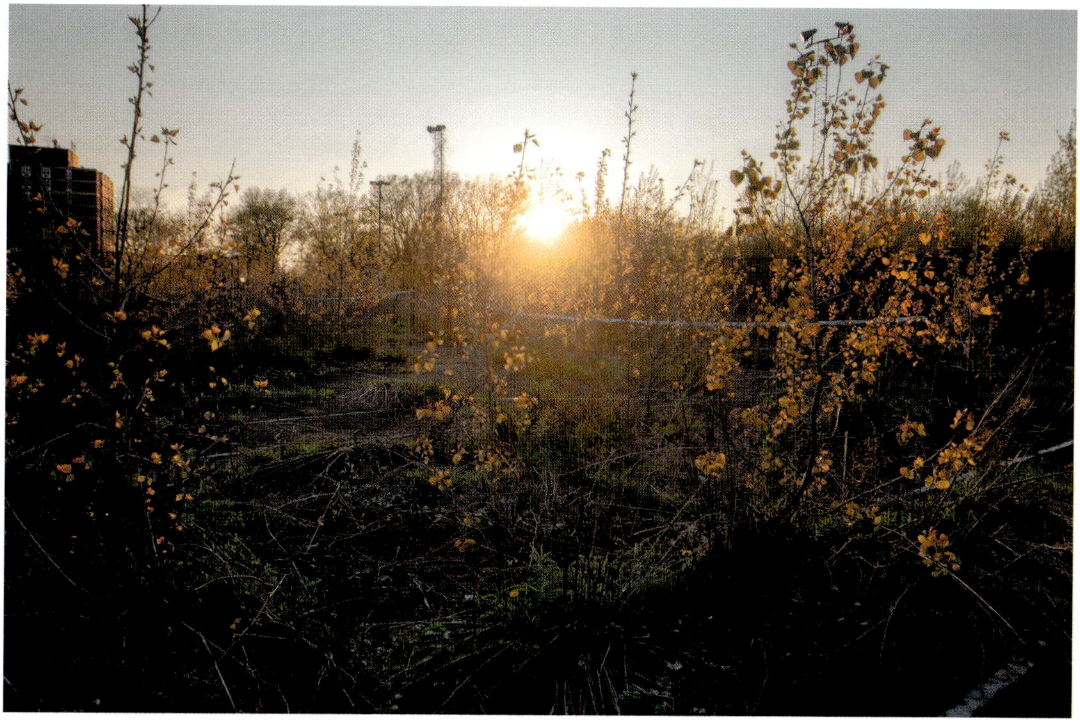

Sun sets over the courts in early summer.

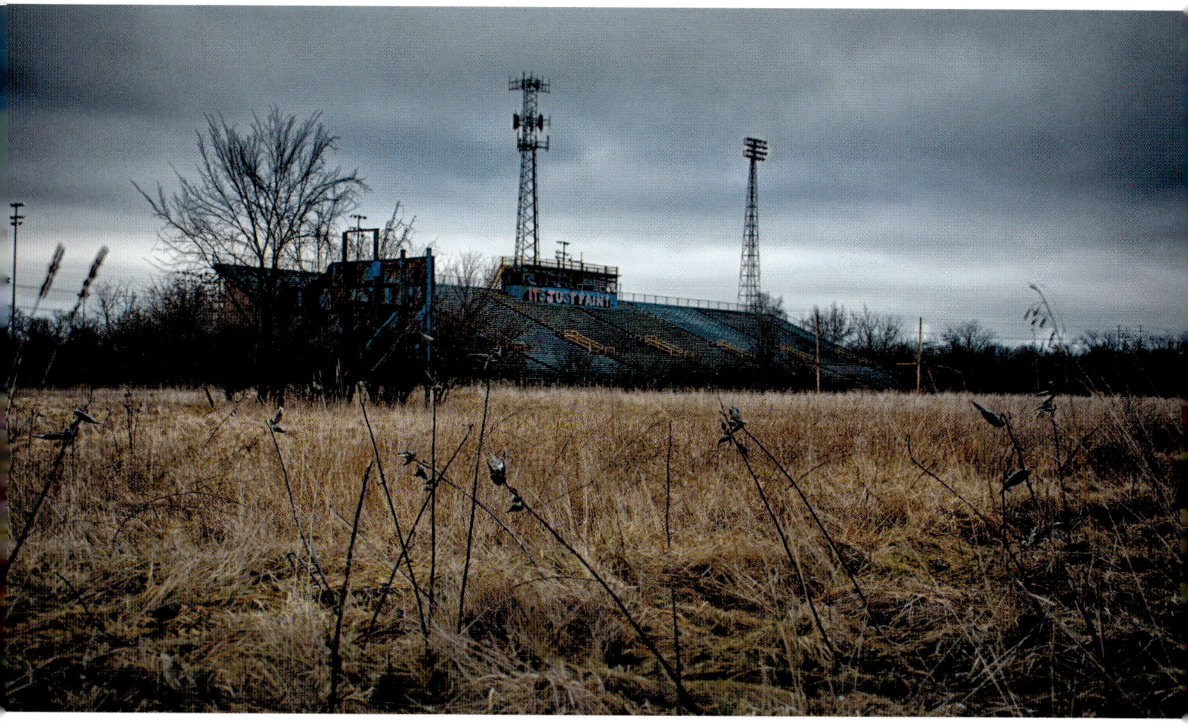

The courts are part of a larger athletic complex which also features a football stadium.

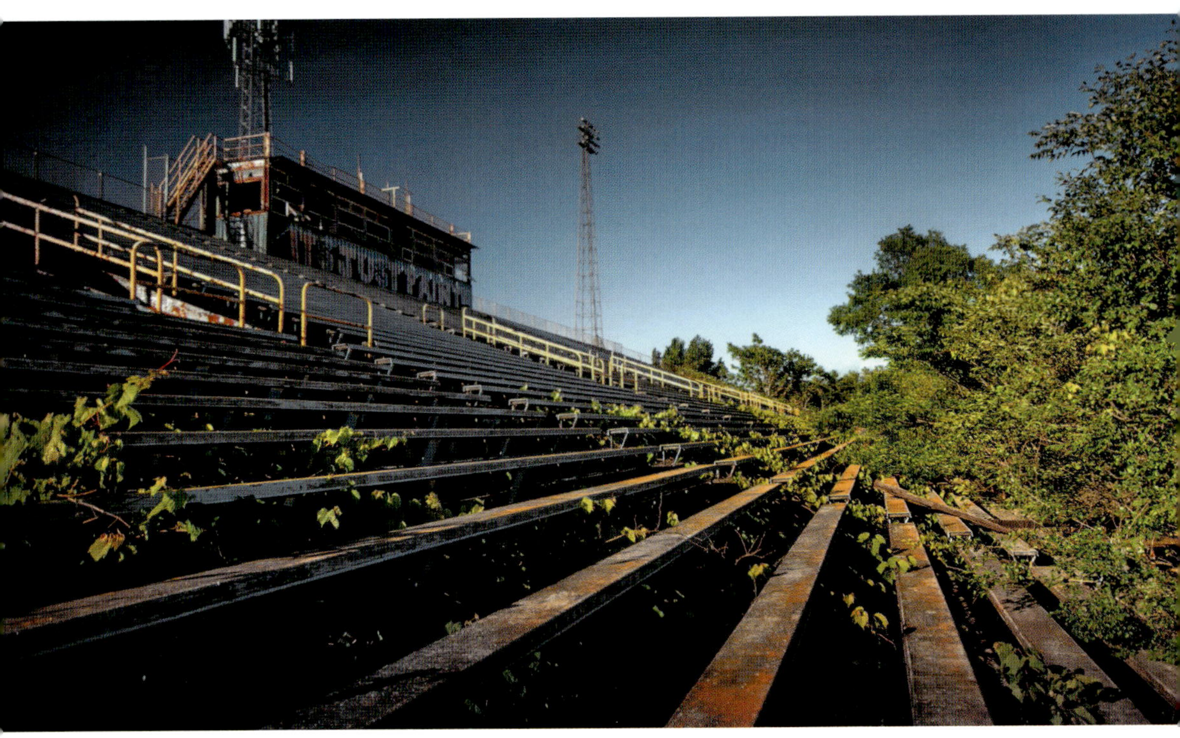

Nature is emboldened.

Shooting these places outside is a reprieve of sorts, a chance to shoot in natural light in all its varieties, relatively safe and on solid ground. For myself, it feels somewhat like a chance to play-act at being a travel photographer, as if I were shooting strange sights in distant lands, rather than in my own back yard. But sooner or later comes time to pack up your gear and head inside. Old buildings give up their secrets reluctantly, and seldom are they on their outside. After all, reprieves are temporary.

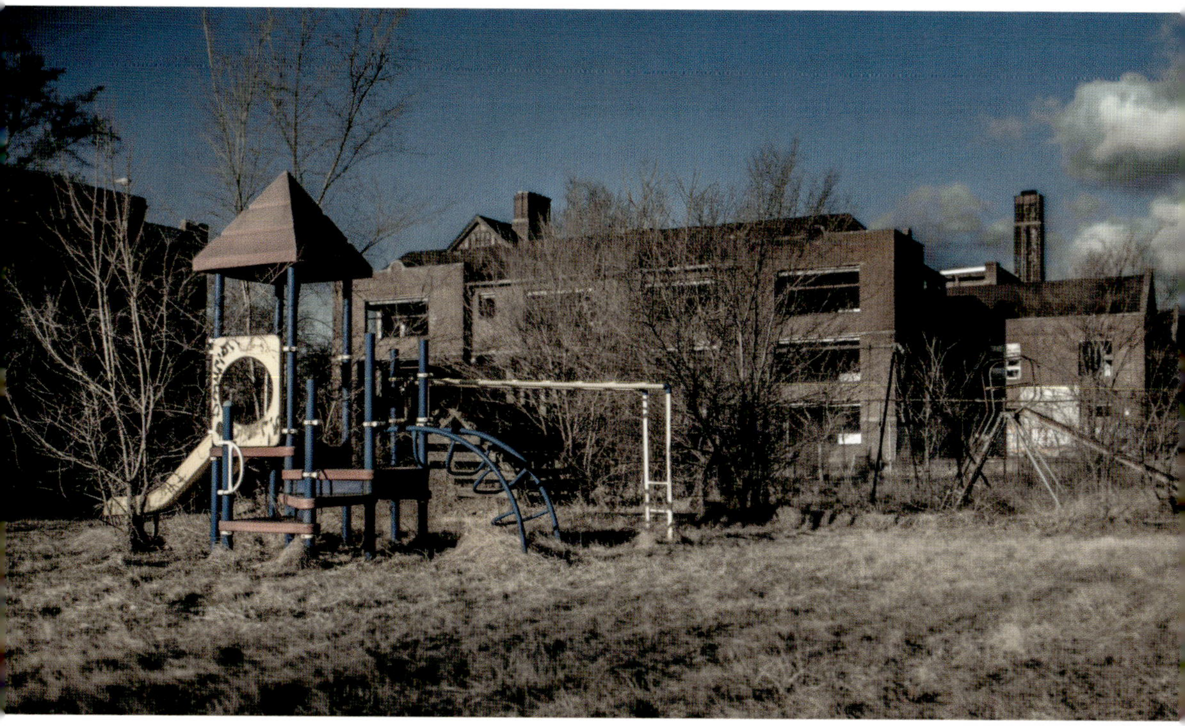

This playground sits outside of a Gary school.

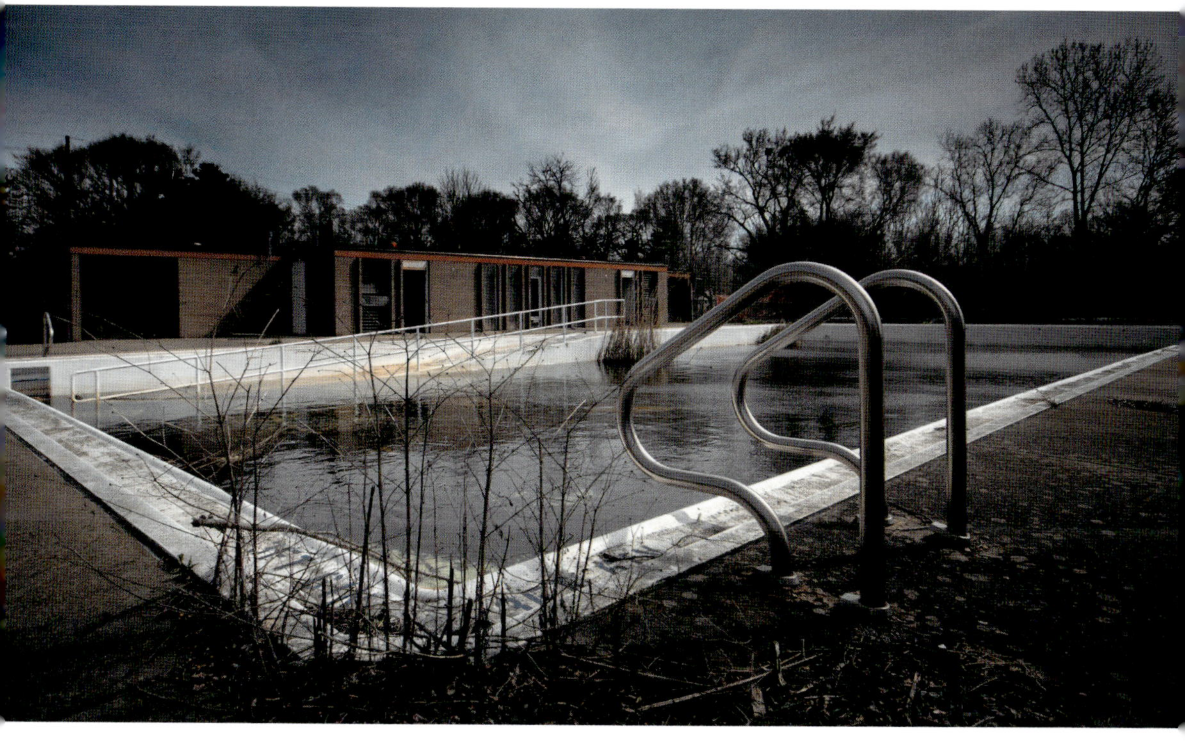

The water is fine.

3

GRAND SPACES

Once inside, it's likely the explorer finds themselves in gloom. Abandoned buildings are often sealed up, either by the last owner or local authorities, and their front doors are rarely open. The "unofficial" way in will often lead to murky basements or darkened hallways, with only a flashlight to show the way. But this sets the stage for one of the joys of urban exploration: the big reveal. It's the moment upon reaching the top of some stairs or rounding a corner to suddenly find yourself in a vast hall, and it can be breathtaking.

These are the spaces where masses of people would congregate, usually for work, play, or worship, and are often the areas that the explorer will photograph first once inside. They are typically some of the most well-lit interiors to explore, and the interplay of the streaming sunlight with the grand geometries of the spaces themselves will invite the photographer to spend the lion's share of their time within them. They can be challenging to shoot, as their sheer size means there is a vast number of possible angles and framings. Often these spaces get photographed in a very symmetrical one-point perspective, and the resulting images looking like the potential setting for an apocalyptic Wes Anderson film. In any case, a good wide-angle lens is invaluable here to capture the expanses.

Church interiors are most emblematic of these kinds of grand spaces. Their very architecture, with their high ceilings and altars, is meant to awe and inspire. This quality seldom fades after abandonment, though it may change in tone. Whatever beliefs were preached inside these churches during their lives, their message becomes something more universal after their abandonment as decay sets in.

The First Methodist Church of Gary is, for good and bad, an open secret among explorers today. It is hard to miss the crumbling edifice while driving past, and access to the interior has always been easy. If I had any illusions that this was a spot only known to a select few area photographers, they were dispelled some years back when, while up the street unpacking the gear from my trunk, an eager and fresh-faced kid came up and asked me if I was there for the big photo meet-up. Regardless, a spot's popularity doesn't diminish its photogenic qualities, any more than Beethoven's allure has faded by dint of being performed thousands of times in the past two centuries. I've still been here more times than I can count; though I've photographed this thing to death, I never tire of this wonder of stone and sky.

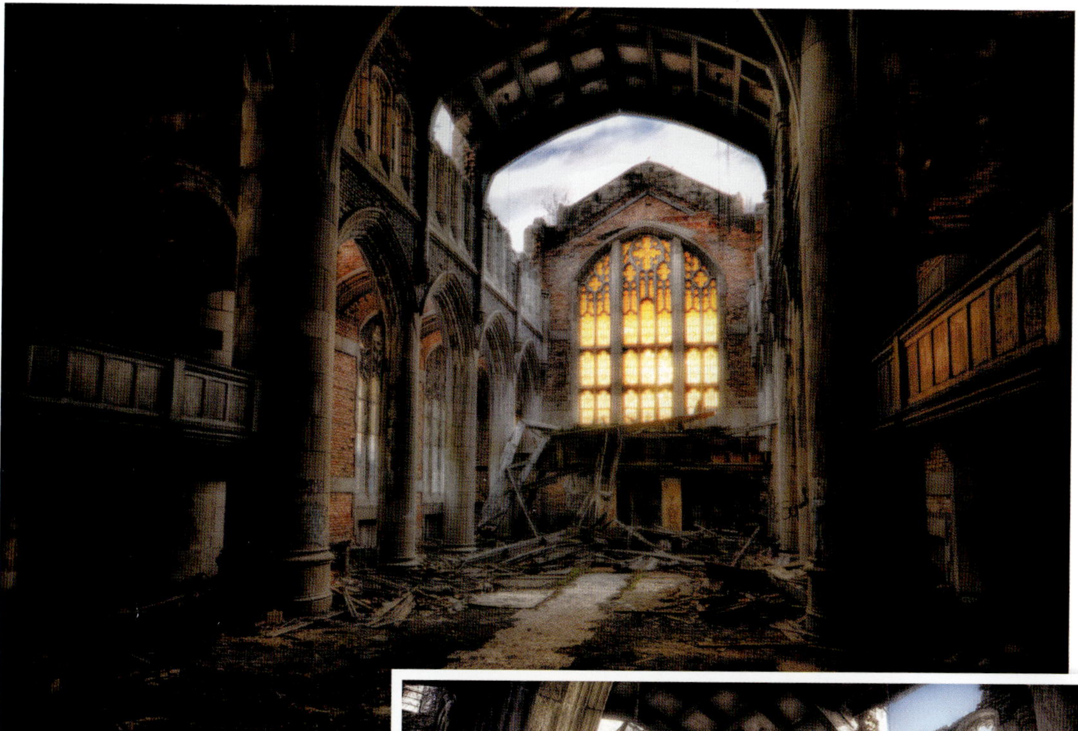

Above: This sight was my first "oh, wow" moment in urbex.

Right: These Romanesque details hide any number of great views.

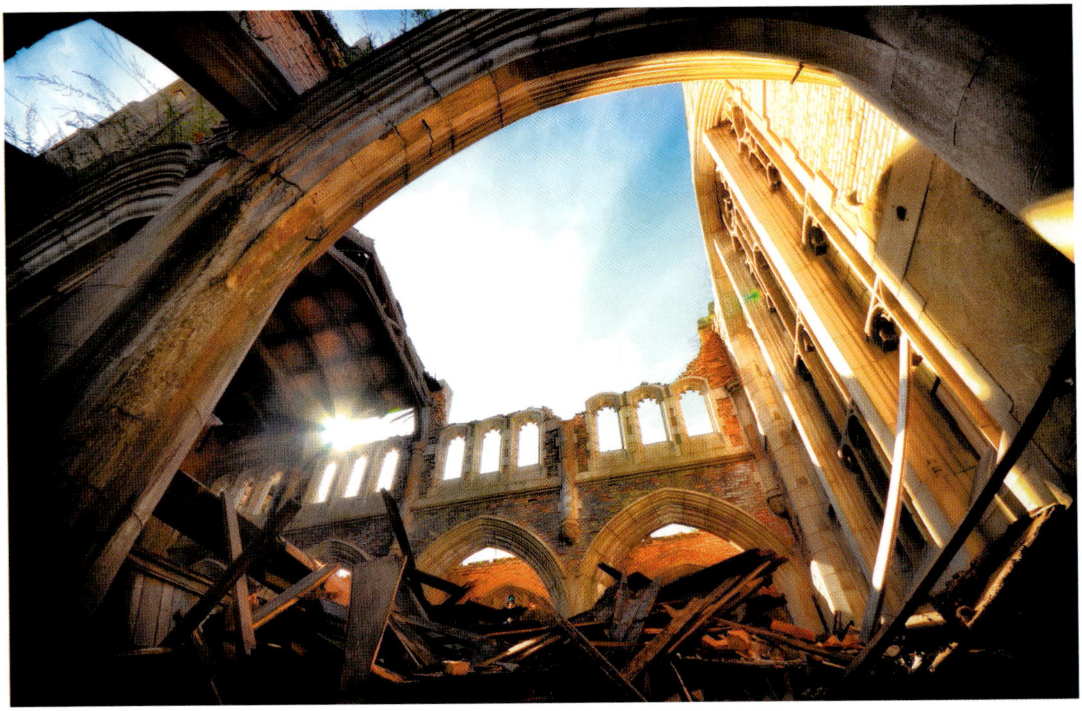

Sunlight fills the front of the church and collapsed balcony.

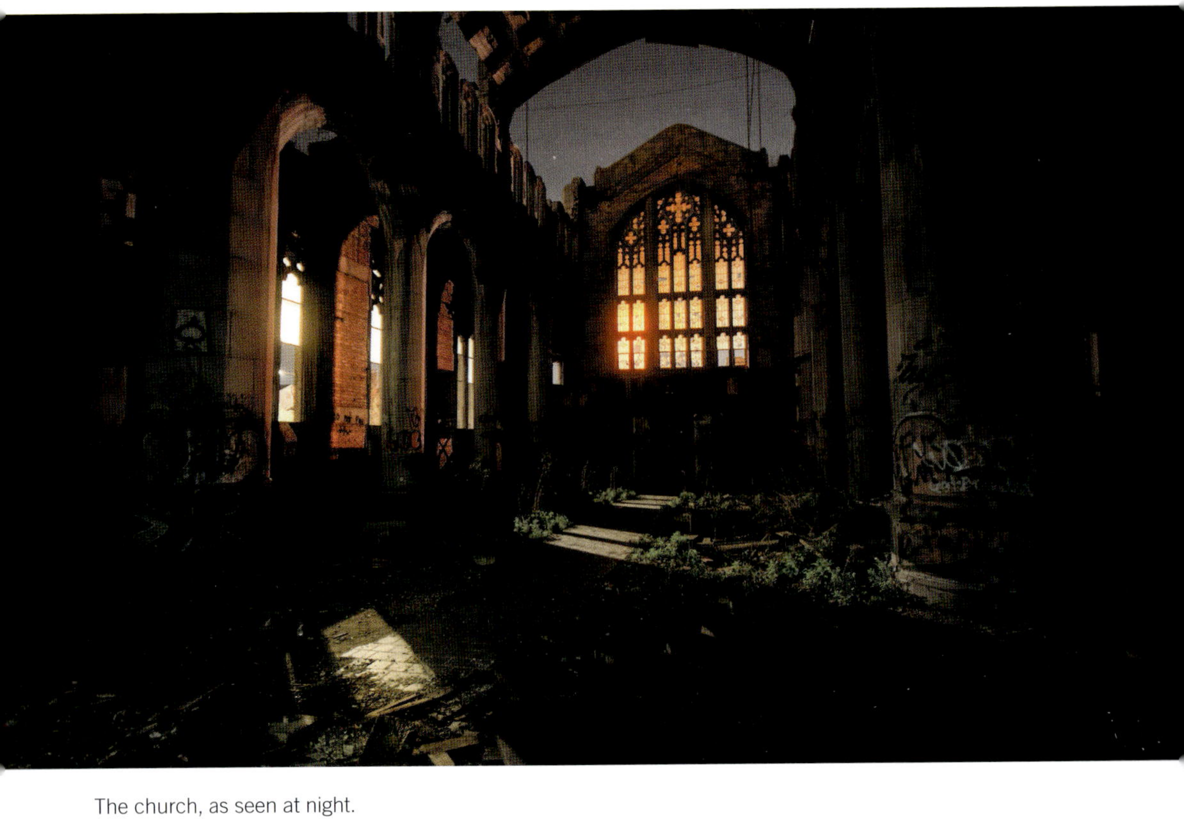

The church, as seen at night.

The church below no longer exists; I shot it during demolition while the building was quite literally cut in half. Its story was likely that of many other Catholic churches on Chicago's south side. Immigrant communities would anchor themselves around a house of worship that they themselves would raise funds for and build in their neighborhoods. This would become the focal point of the community for generations. South siders would ask new acquaintances which parish they were from, rather than what neighborhood or suburb. White flight would drive the original congregation out to the suburbs, and sometimes a different Catholic ethnicity would take over. Eventually, though, the huge buildings would become home to a Black Baptist or Pentecostal church. Then, when even they couldn't afford the mortgage or the upkeep on the crumbling buildings, they would reach their final stage: abandoned and waiting for the wrecking ball. And that is how we found Saint Lawrence church mid demolition.

I visited this church on an unusually warm Christmas Eve. Though at some point arsonists had tried to burn it down, it seems the fire fizzled out, leaving some charred furniture and a sooty interior. How the windows remained so clear, I'll never know.

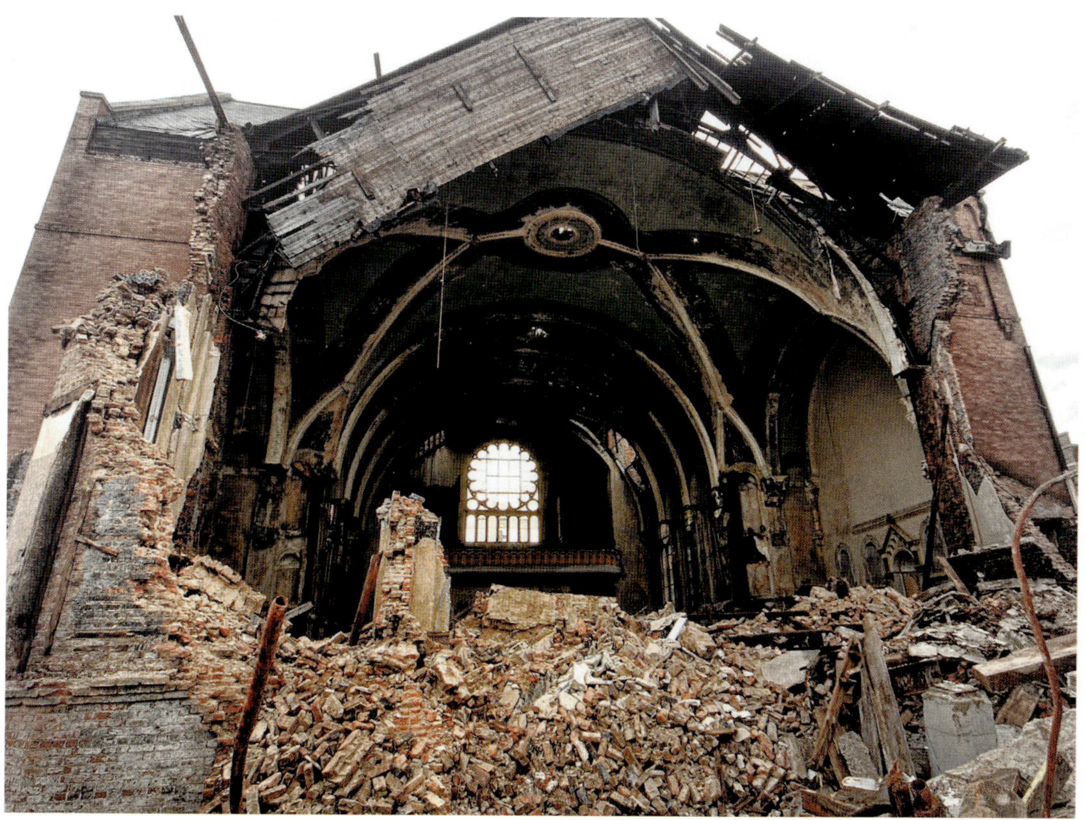

The approach to St. Lawrence church was pile of rubble.

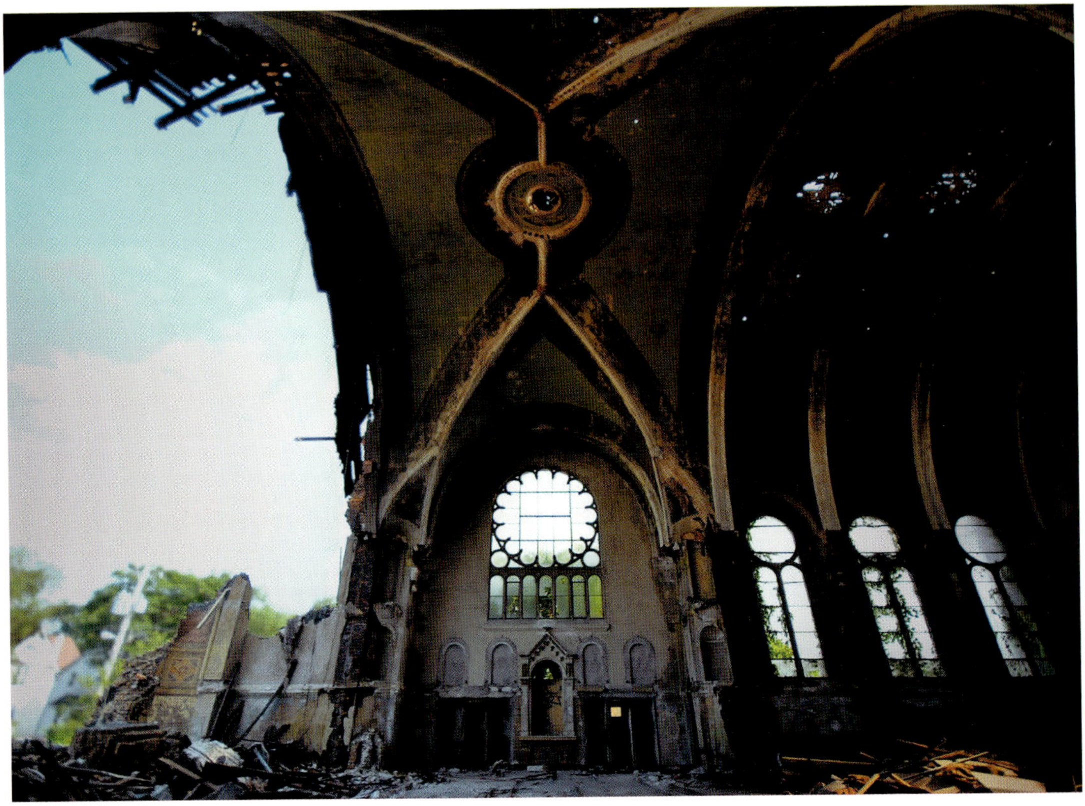

Jesus wept.

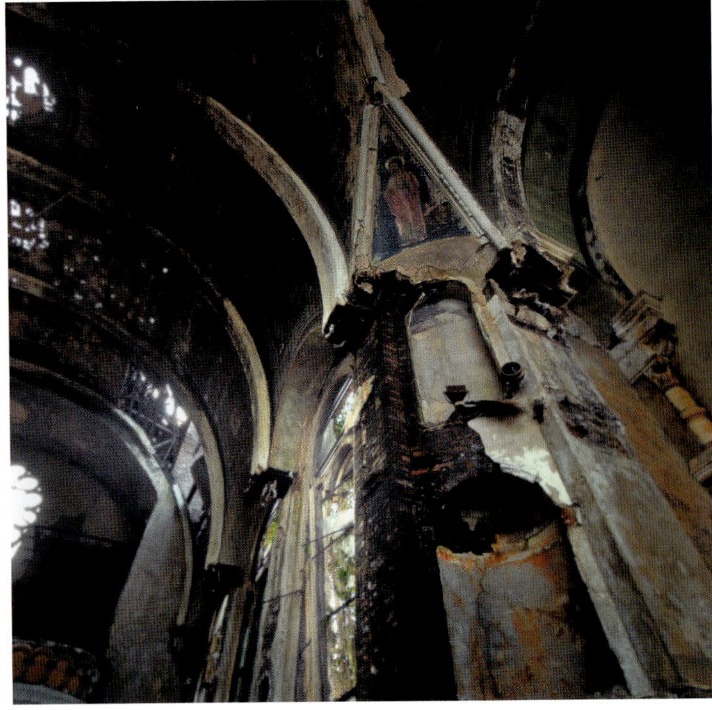

The interior was unused to such qualities of daylight.

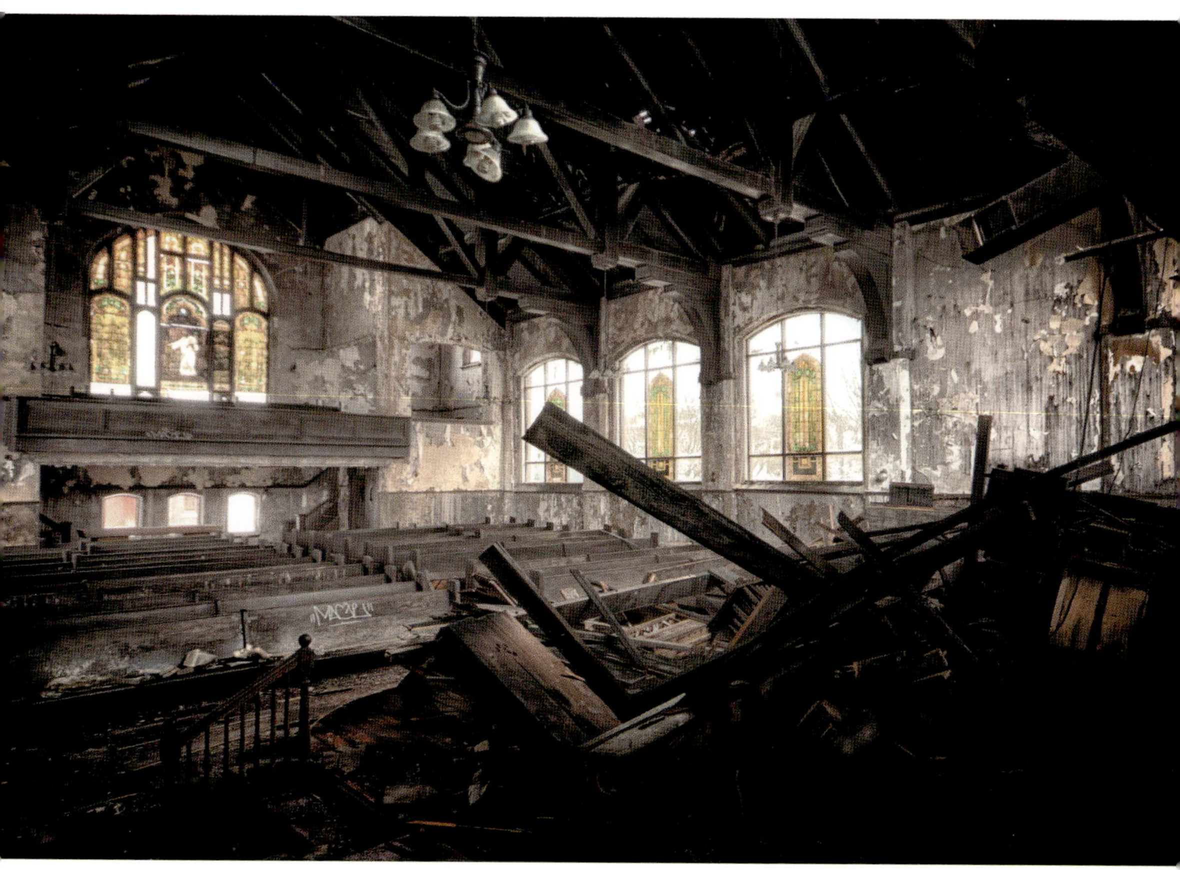

Arson was likely a result, rather than the cause, of the church's closure.

This beautiful temple was originally a Church of Christ Scientist, and drew its architectural inspiration from that faith's mother church in Boston. As such, it has the latter's Byzantine, Ottoman, and Neoclassical style elements. My first visit here ended in a rather humbling fashion, as cracking a rib forced me to give up after having glimpsed just tantalizing bits of the first-floor interior. I had more luck on a subsequent trip, and was able to get in and shoot this magnificent place.

Houses of worship may be the foremost examples of grand, open spaces, but there are many others. Like altars in churches, theaters and auditoriums have stages that are the focal point of these vast rooms, while gyms, factories and hallways can also be striking in their own way. Even a funky modern convent, with its central atrium illuminated by a skylight reminiscent of a disco floor, had a similar vibe.

After this, it's time to delve deeper and discover what else these old buildings hold.

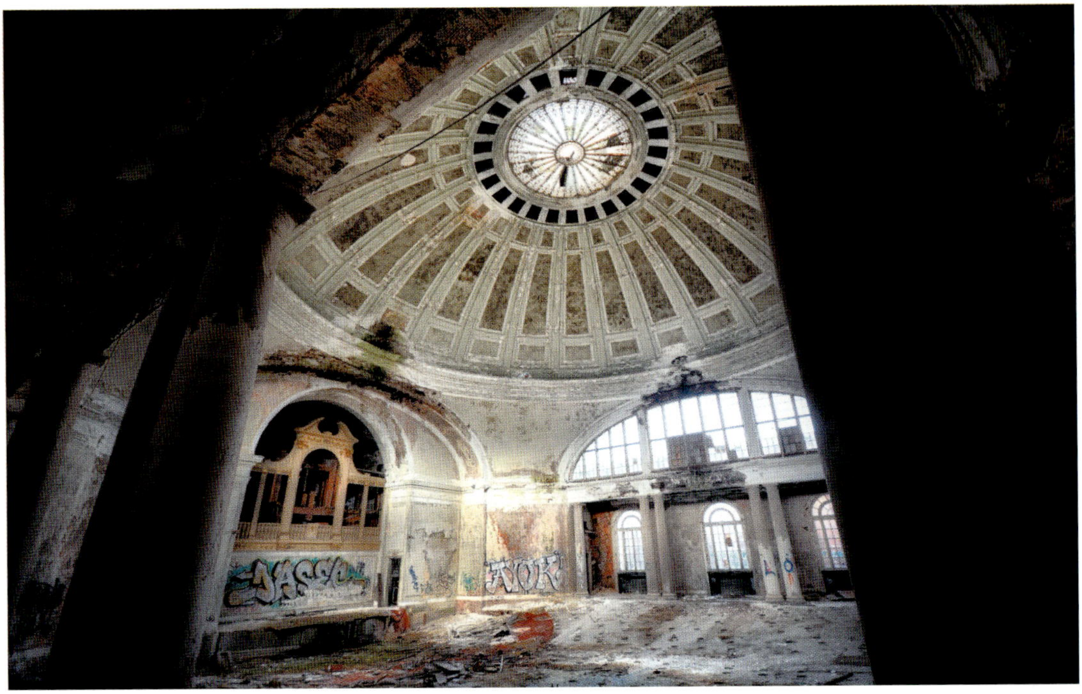

An architectural hodgepodge can make for great urbex.

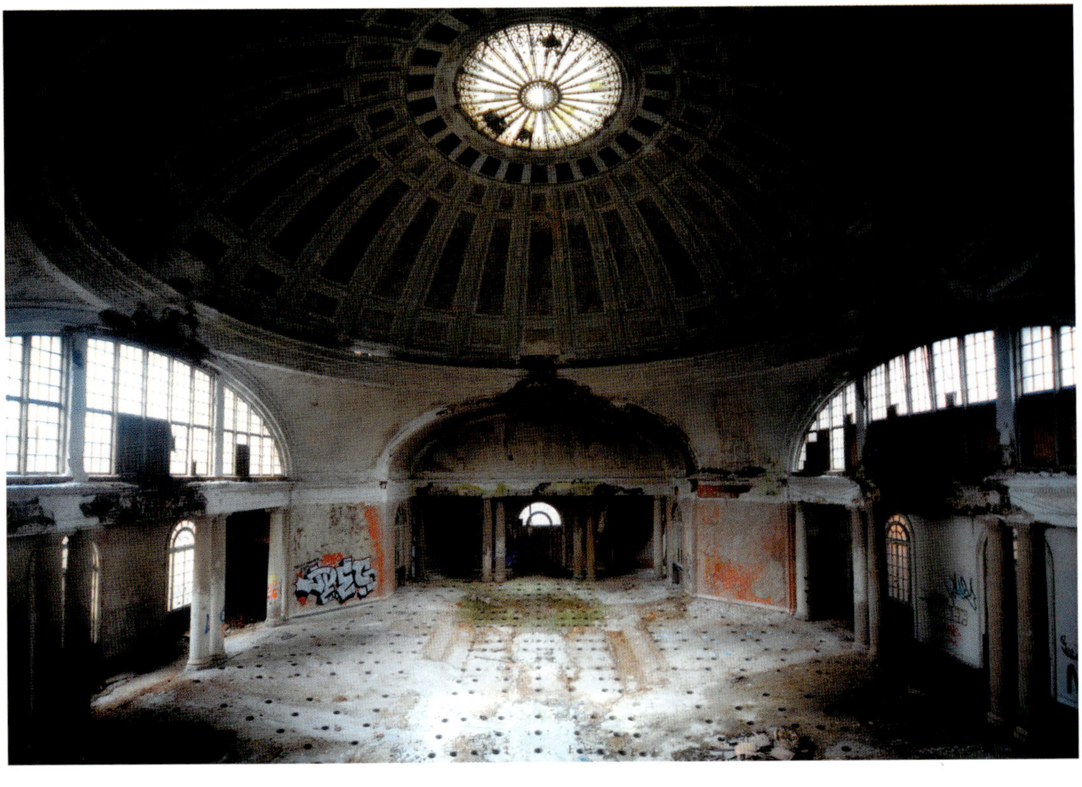

The organist's view looked out over the altar.

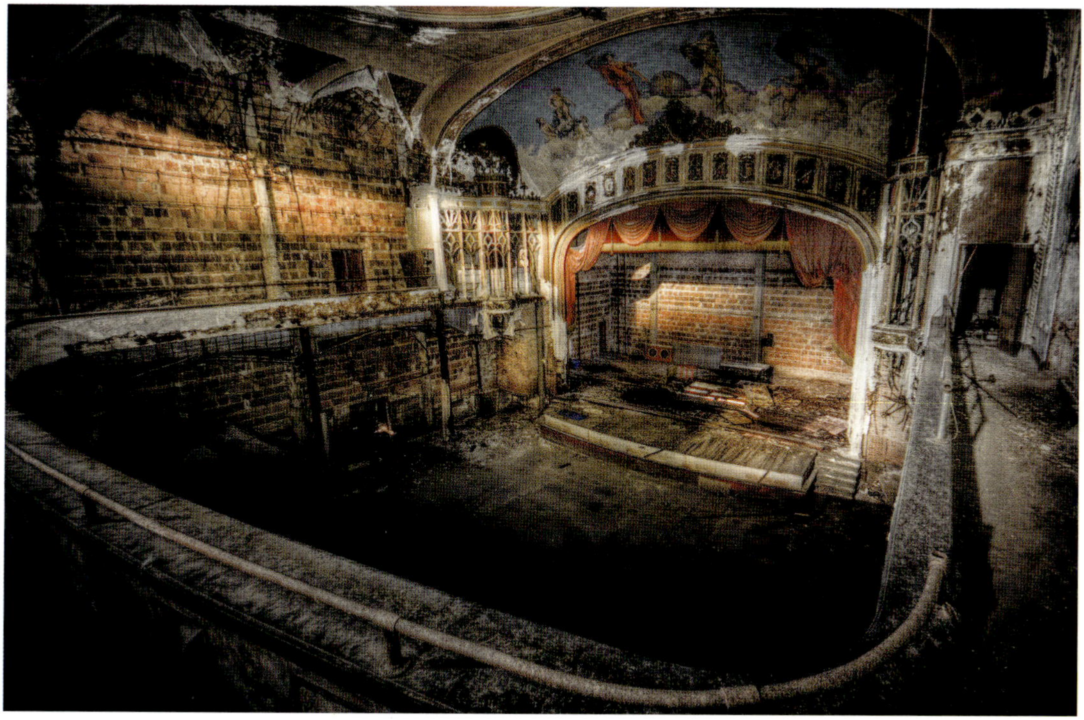

Light hits the stage of derelict theater in far northern suburbs.

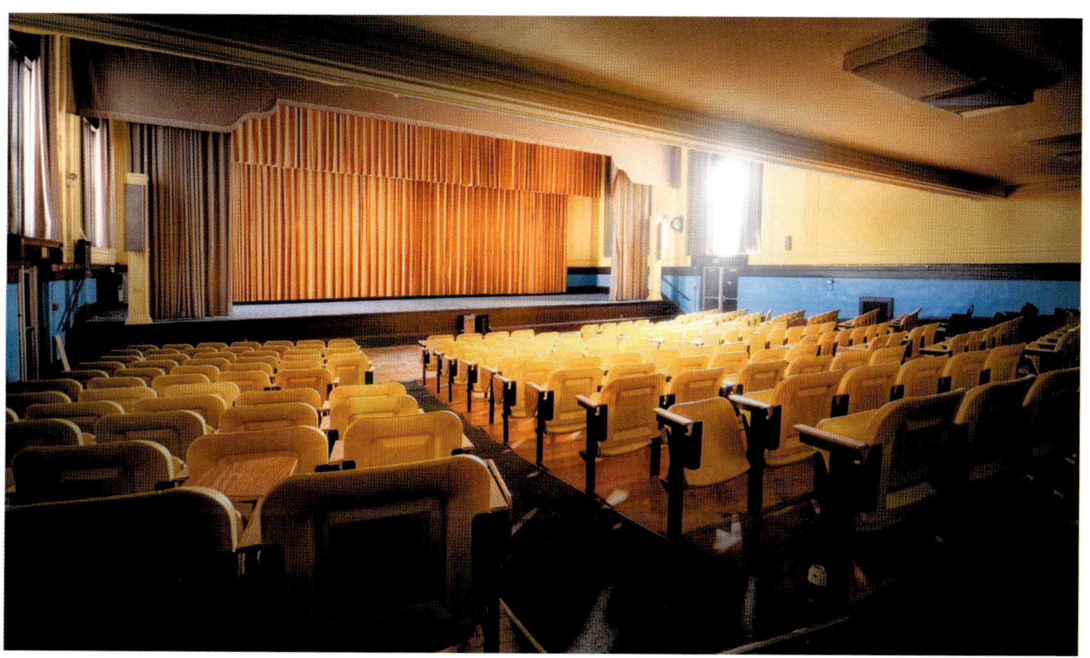

Goldenrod was one of many bold color choices in the interior of this shuttered west side school.

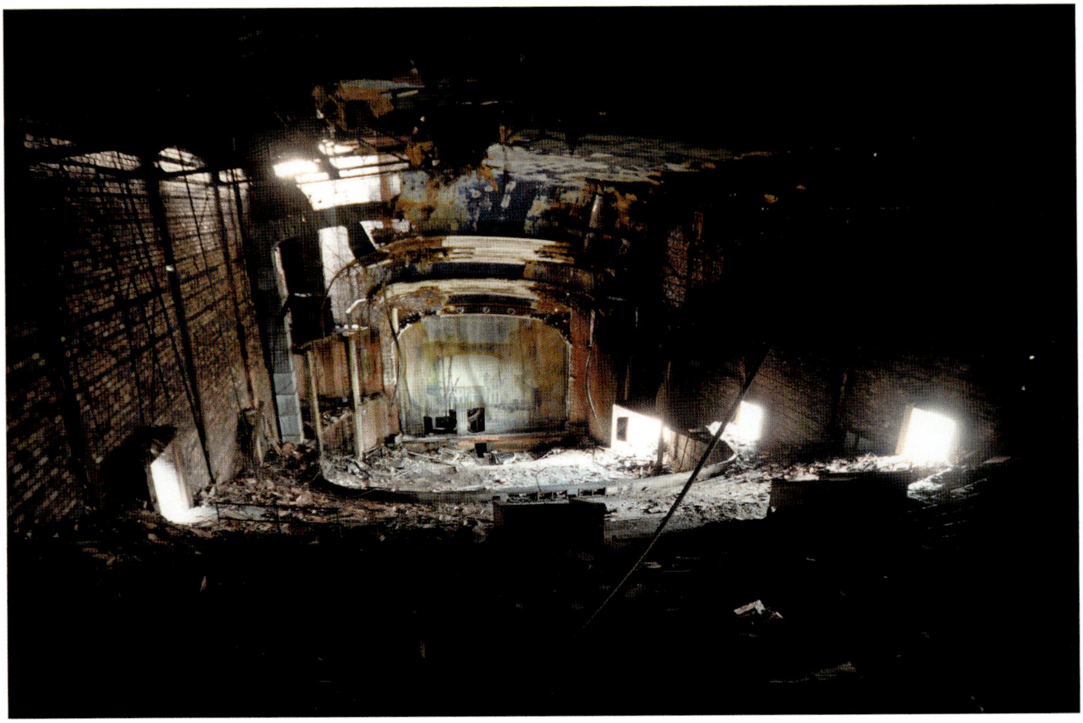

When the gilt, drop ceilings, and plaster fall away, some old theaters are exposed for what they really are: brick boxes.

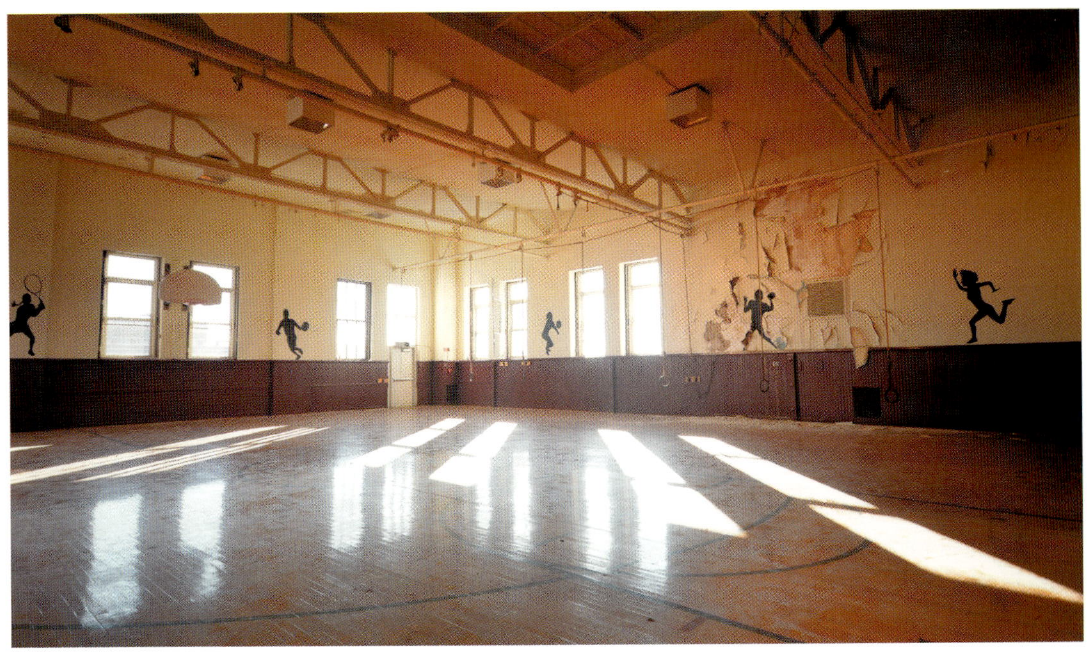

Whimsical silhouettes of kids at play are analogous to a cartoon steer on a hamburger wrapper.

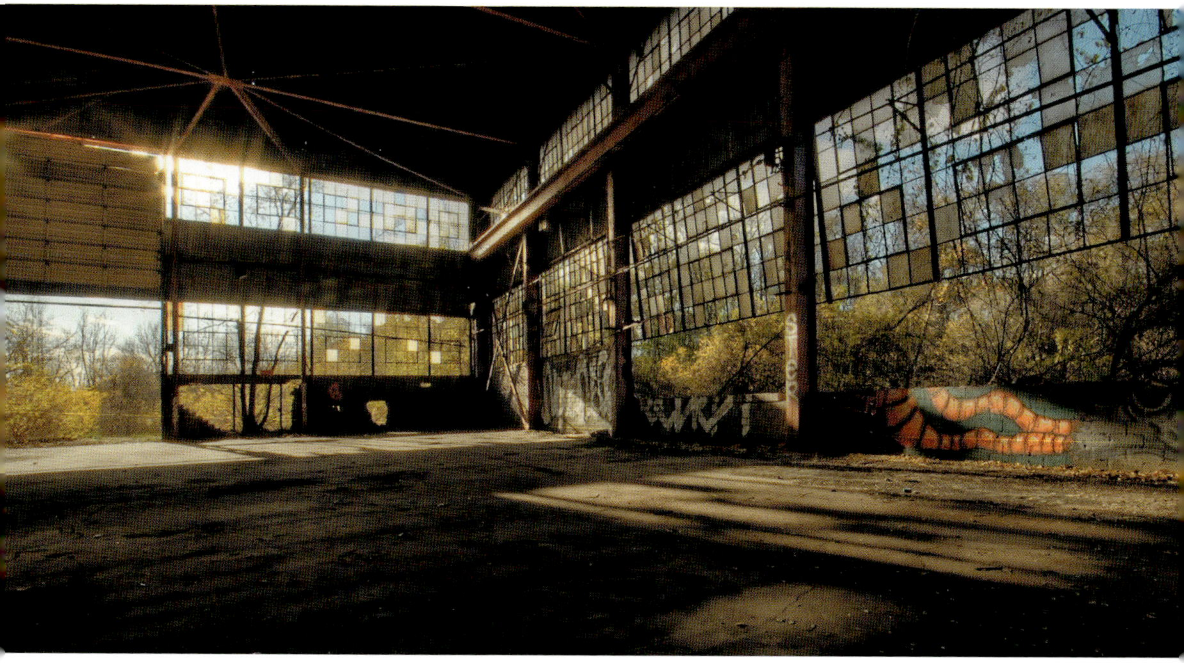

Nature presses in from all sides.

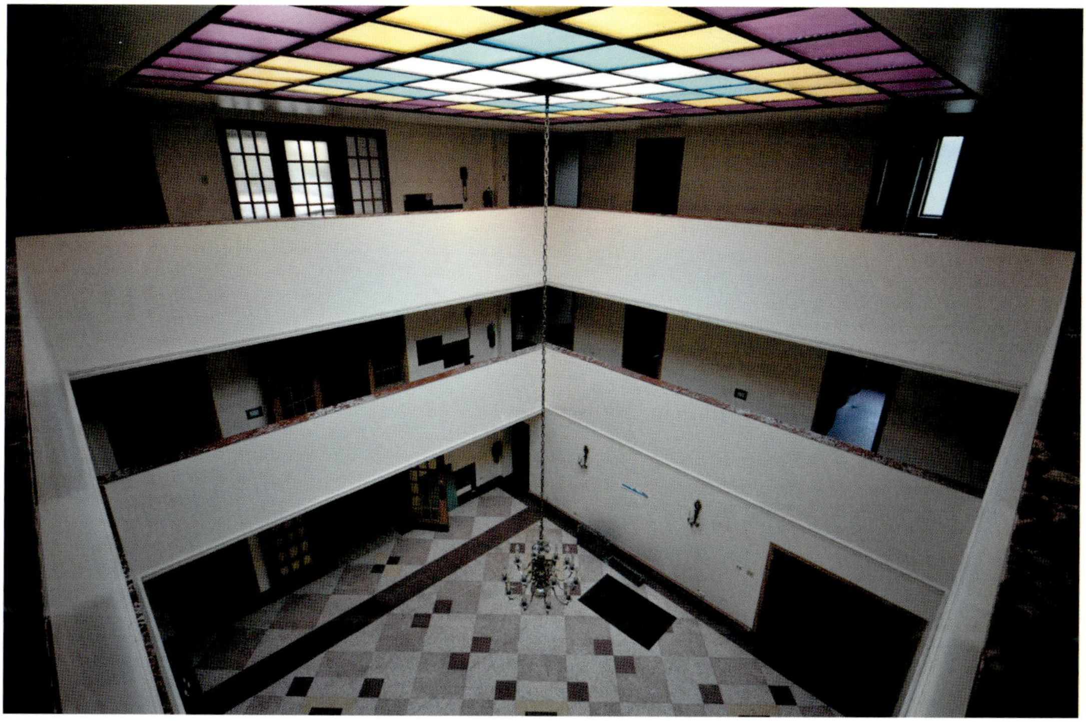

A sober exterior concealed this disco nunnery.

4

GETTING THERE IS HALF THE FUN

Urban exploration is, in a very basic way, about delving into the unknown and forgotten. It is wanting to know what lies behind a rusty door, or what waits at the end of a darkened hallway. Finding this out can be dangerous, and over the years a handful of urbexers have died while many others have sustained serious injuries. Most lethal mishaps tend to be falls. Rooftops are inherently hazardous, but solid-looking floors can be rotted through and give way, or the wrong step in poor light can lead to an open elevator shaft. More decayed buildings can have potentially lethal falling debris, and there are the long-term effects of exposure to molds and asbestos. The most common mishaps aren't deadly but are nonetheless serious; every explorer has stories of cuts and bruises, if not broken bones. I personally have had the experience of driving home with my cupped hand held out of the window as blood slowly pooled and congealed in my palm from a deep gash. More recently, I managed to bash my head against a low beam, and mildly horrified my fellow explorers when I regrouped at our car with blood streaming down my neck. Any scalp wound will bleed profusely, so luckily my injury that day was not as bad as it appeared. I witnessed a good friend of mine step on a manhole cover that had been left askew; it flipped and dropped her into the depths below. Painfully, her elbows and backside broke her fall and held her in place until we frantically pulled her clear. Plunging into mystery can have consequences, and each threshold crossed entails some risk.

Corridors, doorways, and, especially stairs are particularly potent subconscious symbols of transition and ascension. In an urban exploration context, they symbolize all the risks taken on the journey. Whether for these reasons, aesthetic ones, or likely a combination of both, they make for great photography. Most explorers, after all, have a morbid streak that first attracted them to the old and decayed, and, in this genre, a bit of a death wish can be celebrated. Here are the liminal spaces that lead to our fate, whatever it might be that day.

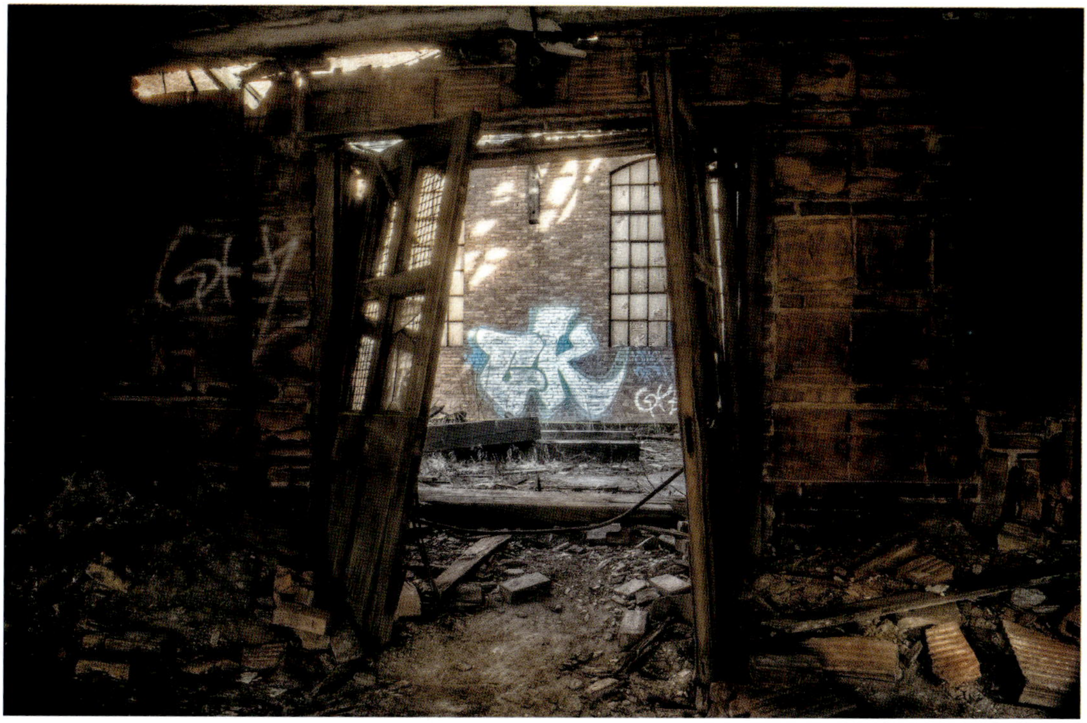

A feeble loved one reaching out for embrace.

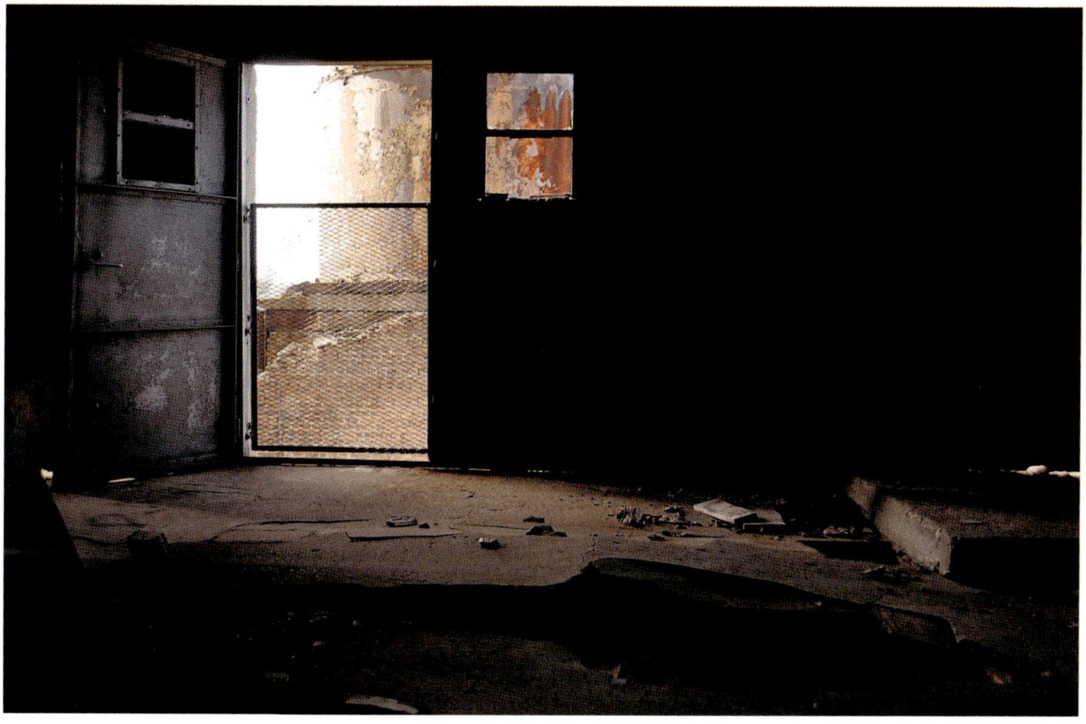

Goth is Noir's dorky little cousin. Thank you for coming to my TED Talk.

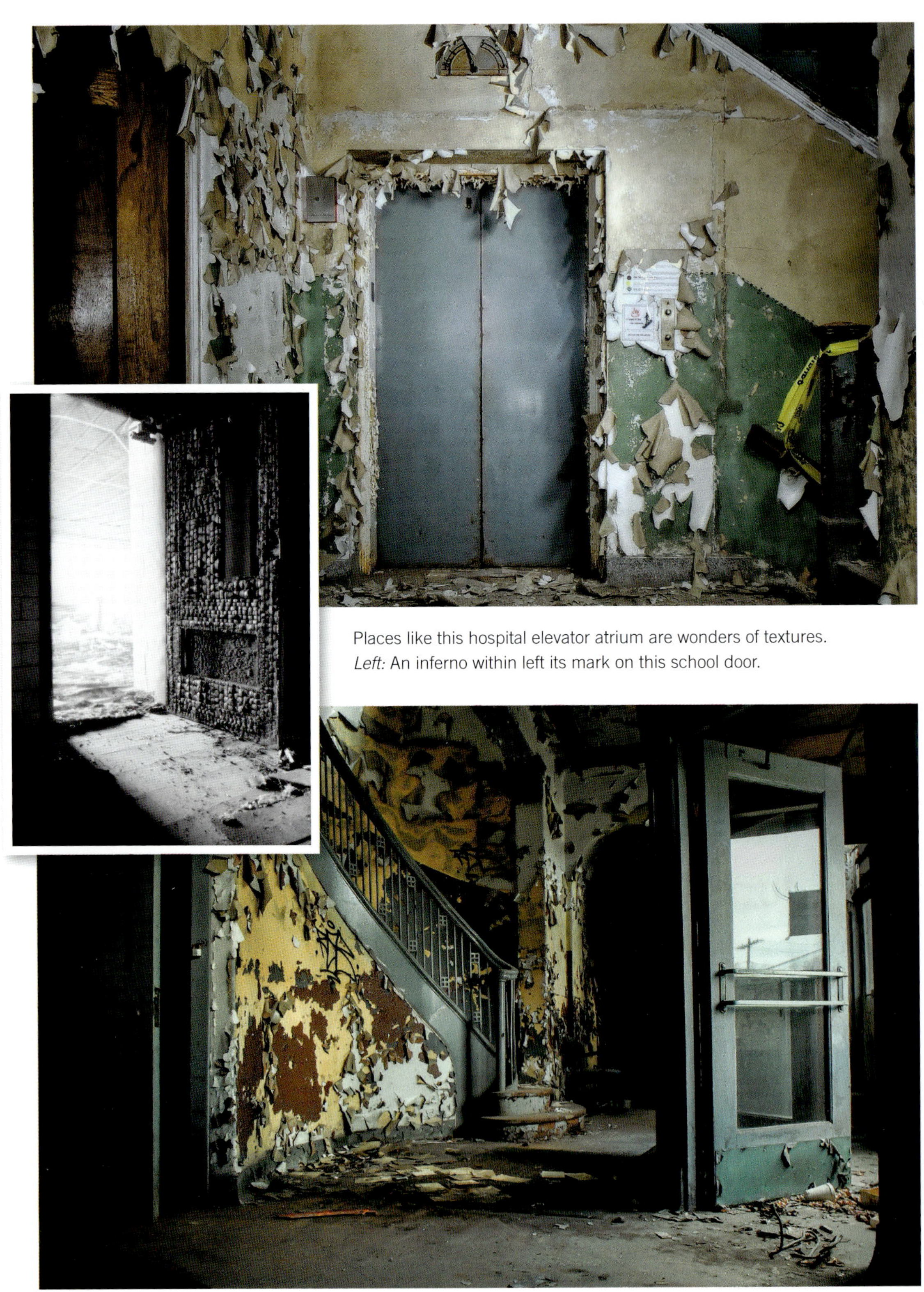

Places like this hospital elevator atrium are wonders of textures.
Left: An inferno within left its mark on this school door.

The walls of a Gary office lobby seem to sizzle as years of layered paint flakes off.

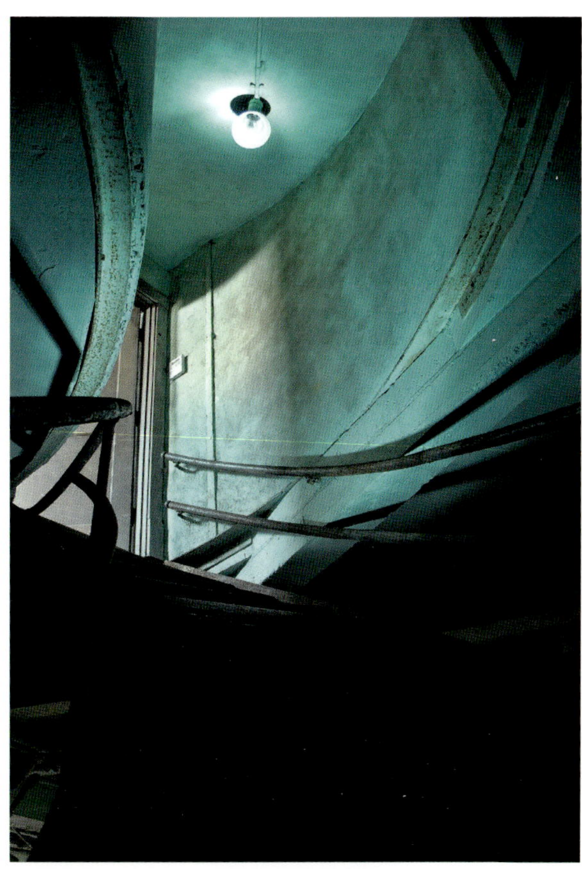

Right: The twisting shapes in this basement staircase triggered a sense of unease.

Below: A piano lies in wait for the incautious explorer.

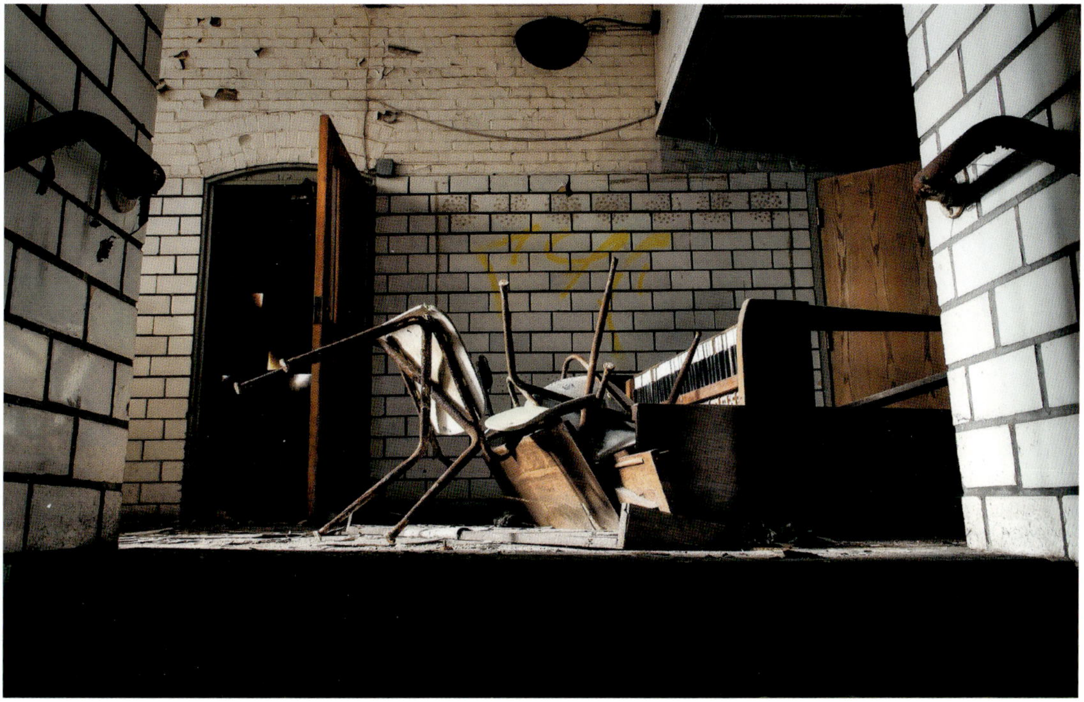

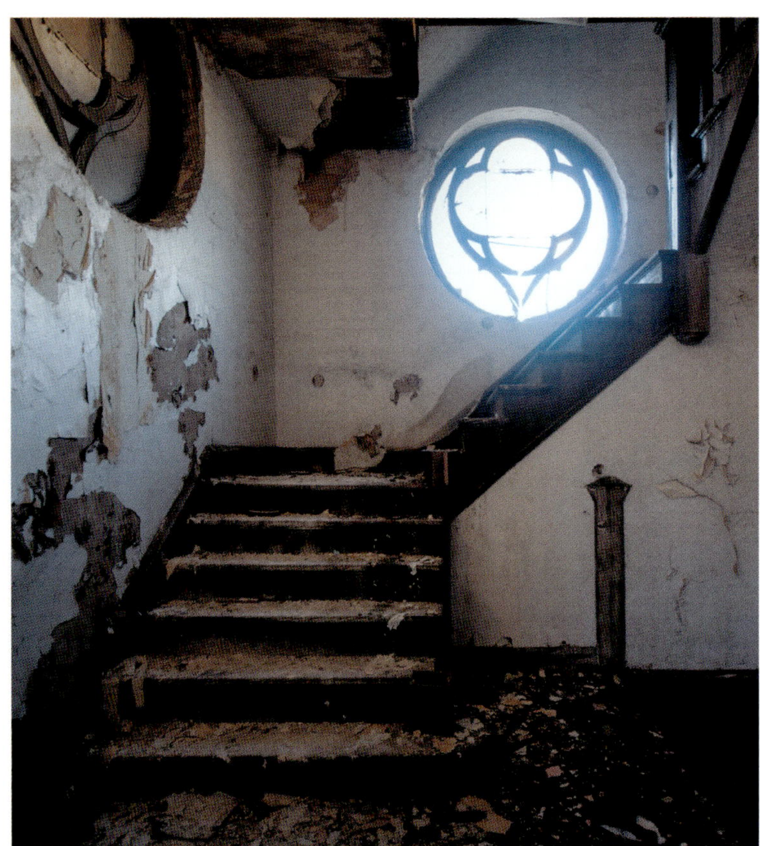

Left: Stairs leading to church belfry.

Below: Newels stand sentry-like at the main entrance stairs of a Chicago school.

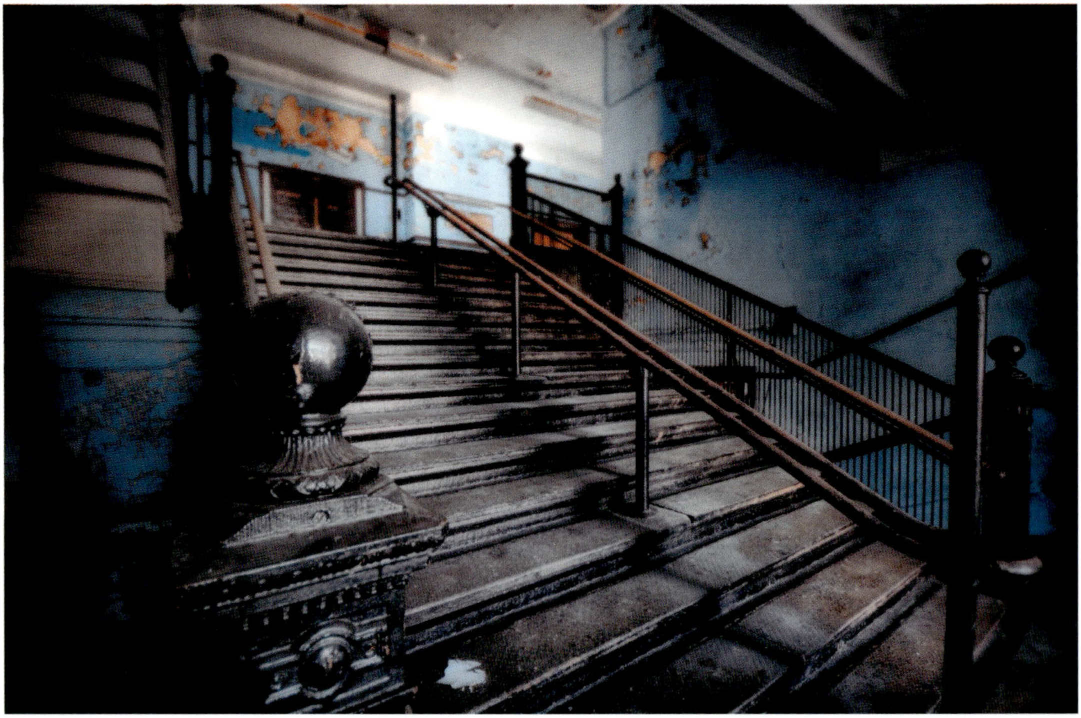

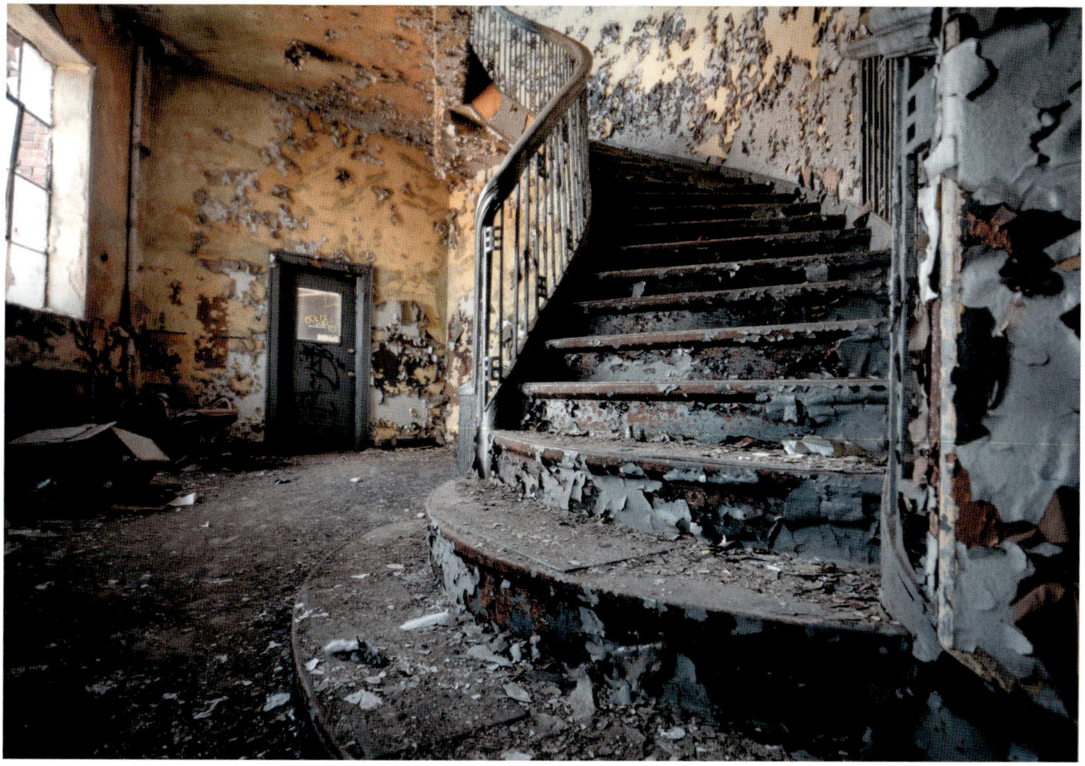

In extreme cases, the frantic textures of peeling paint provide a reasonable approximation of the hallucinatory effects of LSD.

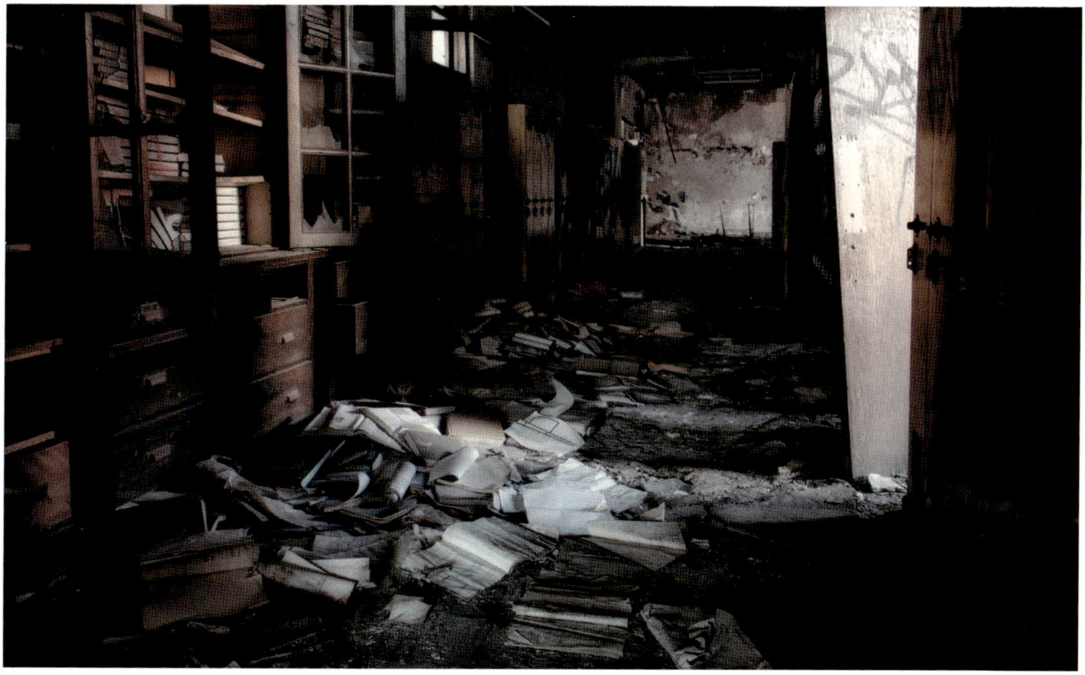

Grey winter's light spills into a parochial school hallway.

5

TABLEAUX VIVANTS

Taking pictures of abandonment is primarily still life photography. Apart from bits of debris stirred by gusts of wind, little moves inside dead buildings. Yet, many of these places seem to exude a sense of life. The decay that comes with time, coupled with the damage left by vandals, taggers, or scavengers, can make an impression of great action, as of an image caught mid-explosion.

Because of this, urbex photography in some ways resembles the old art of staging a *tableau vivant*, or "living pictures." A major form of entertainment right up until the advent of broadcast media, *tableaux vivants* were carefully staged and lighted groups of people and props in poses meant to emulate works of art or stage biblical passages. By the late nineteenth century, even erotic stagings became common as well. Sometimes, if there were many, they would be put on vehicles and driven past an assembled audience, akin to parade floats. In these *tableaux* there is a tension between the stillness and quiet of the performers and the pageantry of colors, poses, and allegories within the scene. Likewise ruins, with their riots of colors, textures, and scattered detritus can take on a life-like quality, as if each bit was possessed by a Japanese *kami,* or spirit.

Exploring abandoned places can feel like viewing a procession of these *tableaux*, with each room entered being a distinct scene, complete with its own cast, lighting, and shades of meaning. Former schools are a perfect example of this, as each classroom is a unique composition of desks, books, and debris.

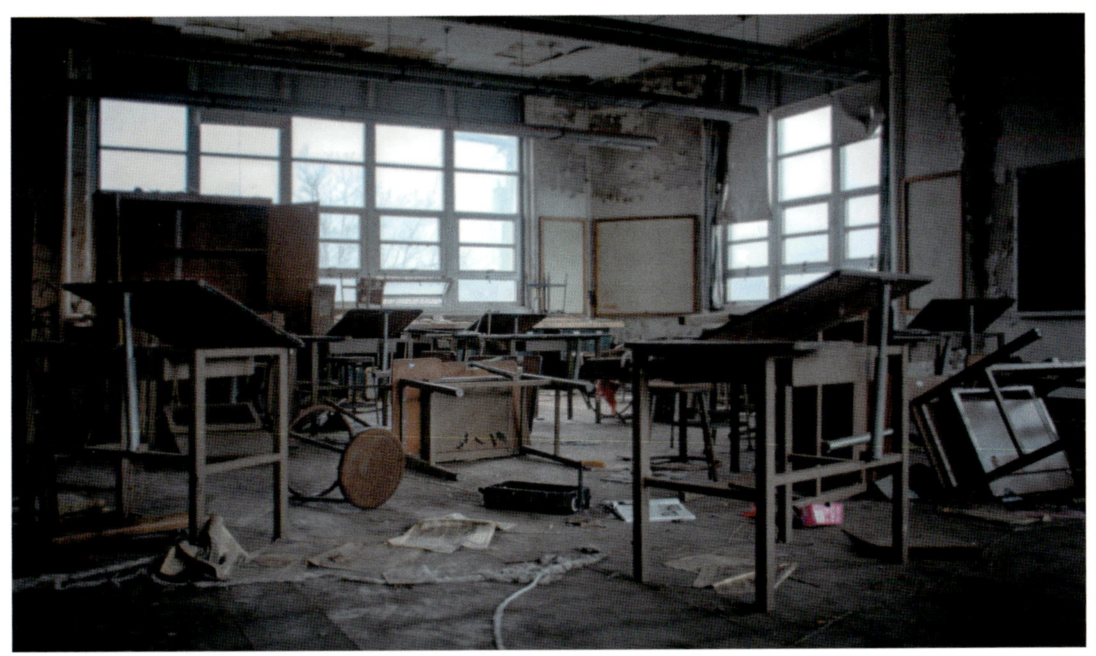

A brawl rages amongst the desks and stools of a drafting classroom.

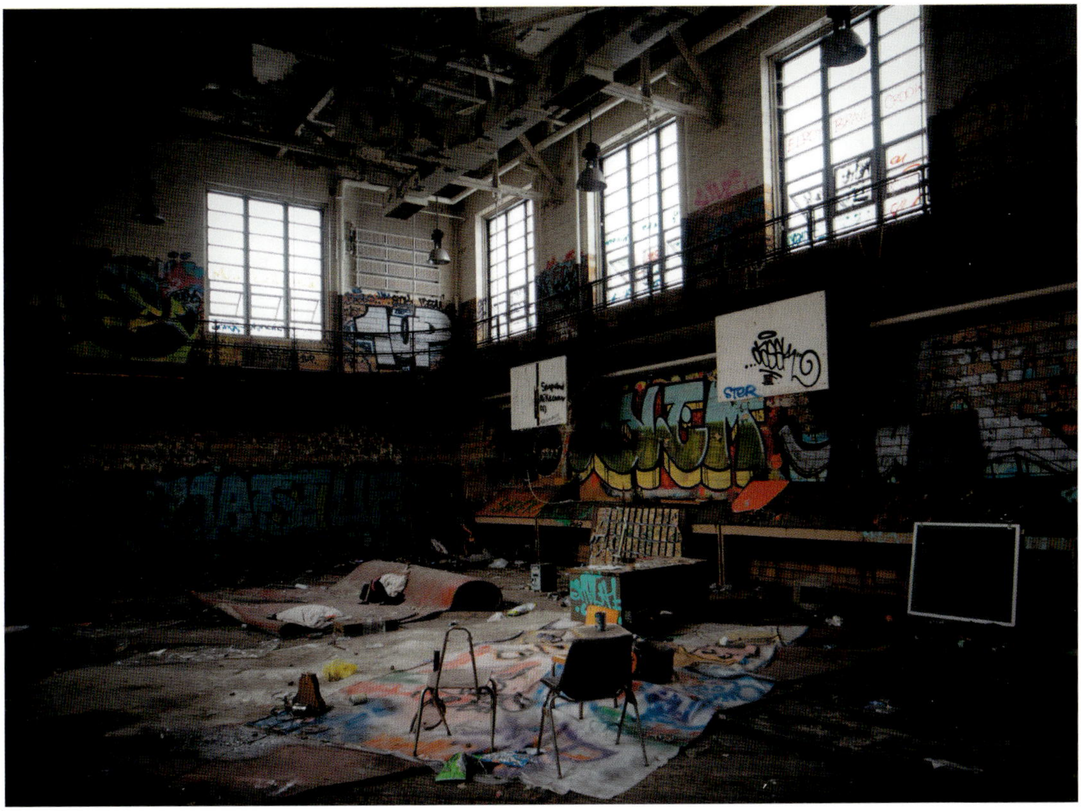

Chairs at the chamber of the four oracles.

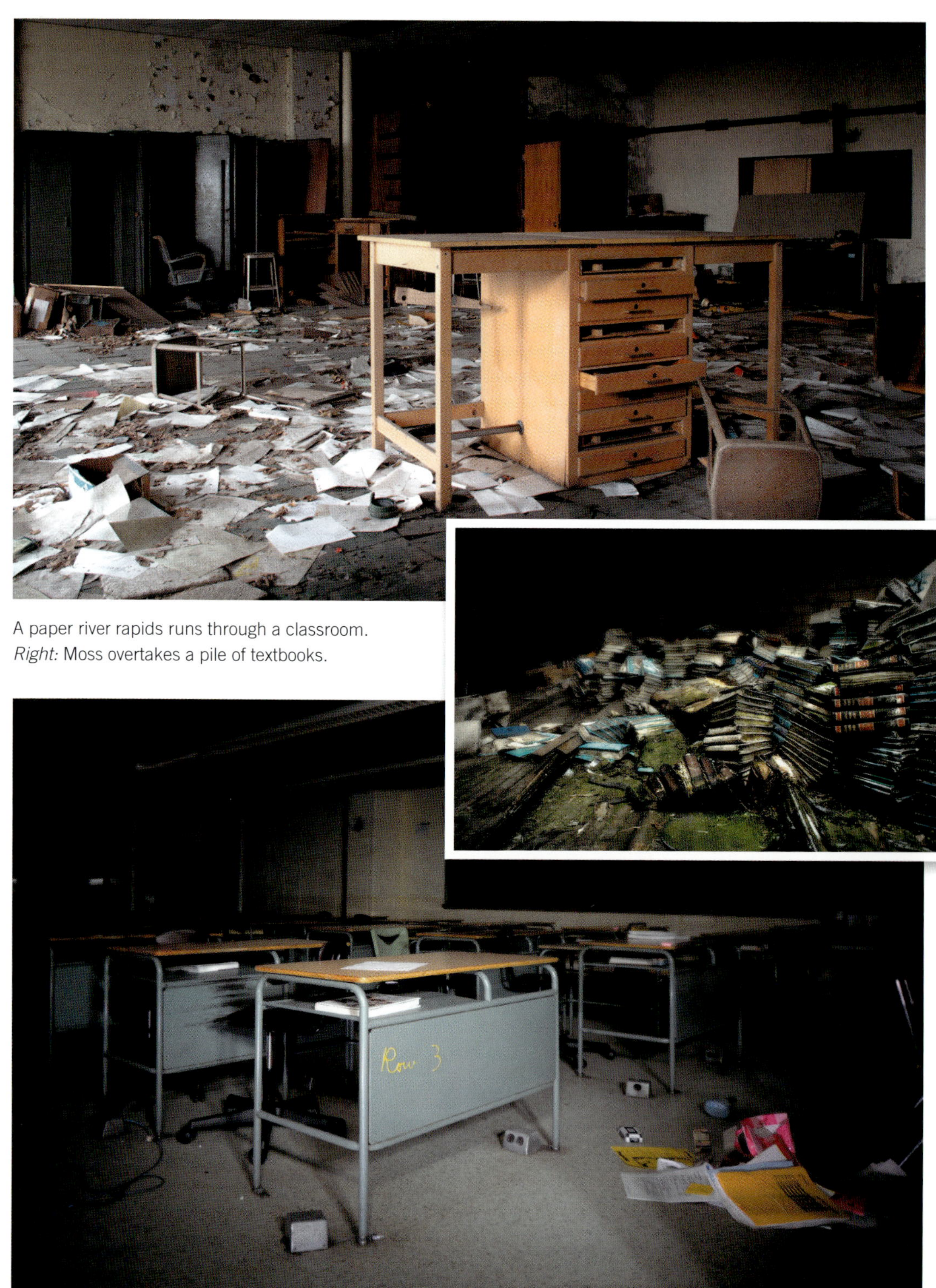

A paper river rapids runs through a classroom.
Right: Moss overtakes a pile of textbooks.

Desks emerge from the gloaming.

A *tableau* like this can be found anywhere enough stuff was left behind. After abandonment, a particular entropy sets in, helped along by previous explorers or others. With time, this chaos blooms into these scenes. Here are examples from some factories and workshops, private homes, and churches. In the last of these, not much evidence for human activity remains. Instead, nature herself has torn through the roof and laid out a thick carpet of moss under the open sky.

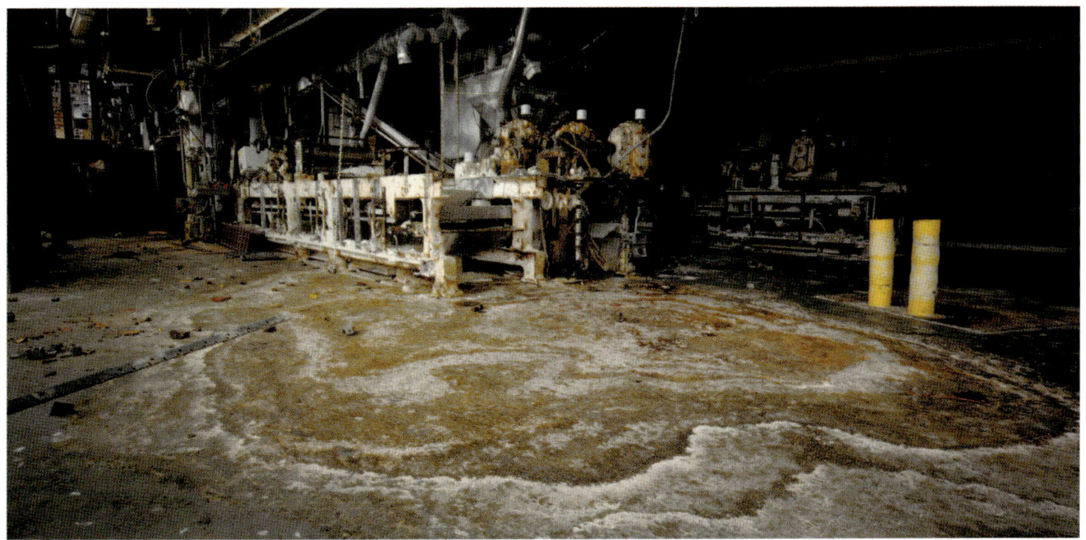

Dried pools of glucose spilled across the floor of this chewing gum plant.

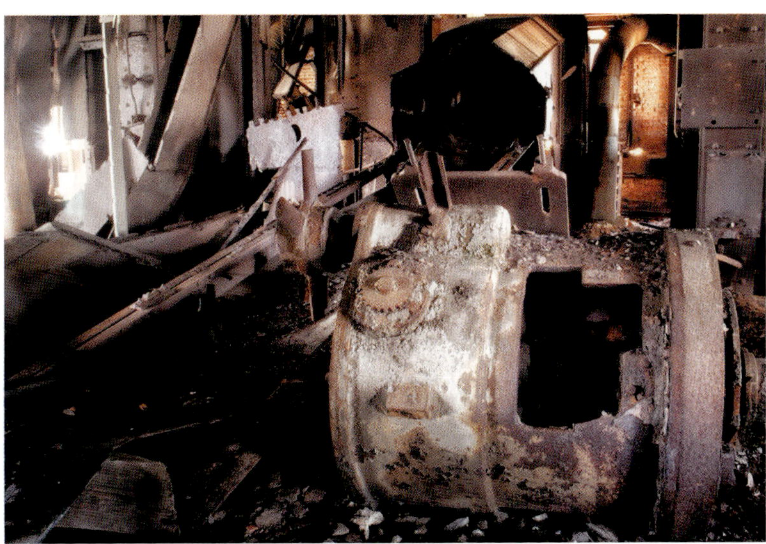

A jumbled scene developed at the conveyor belt.

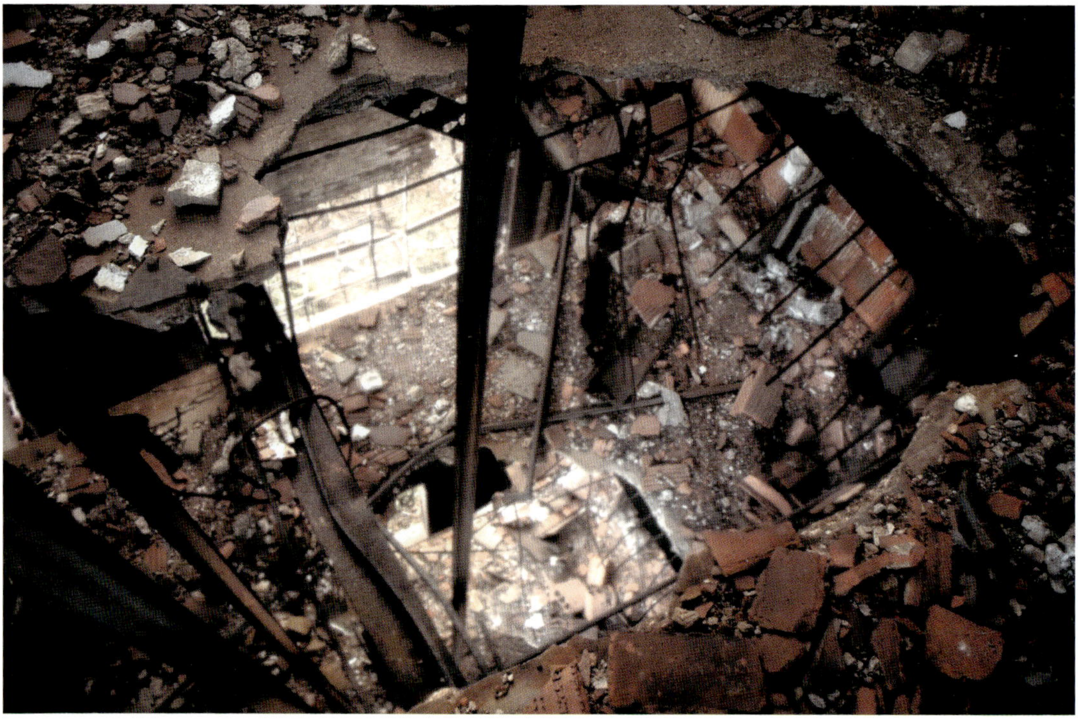

The fastest way is seldom best.

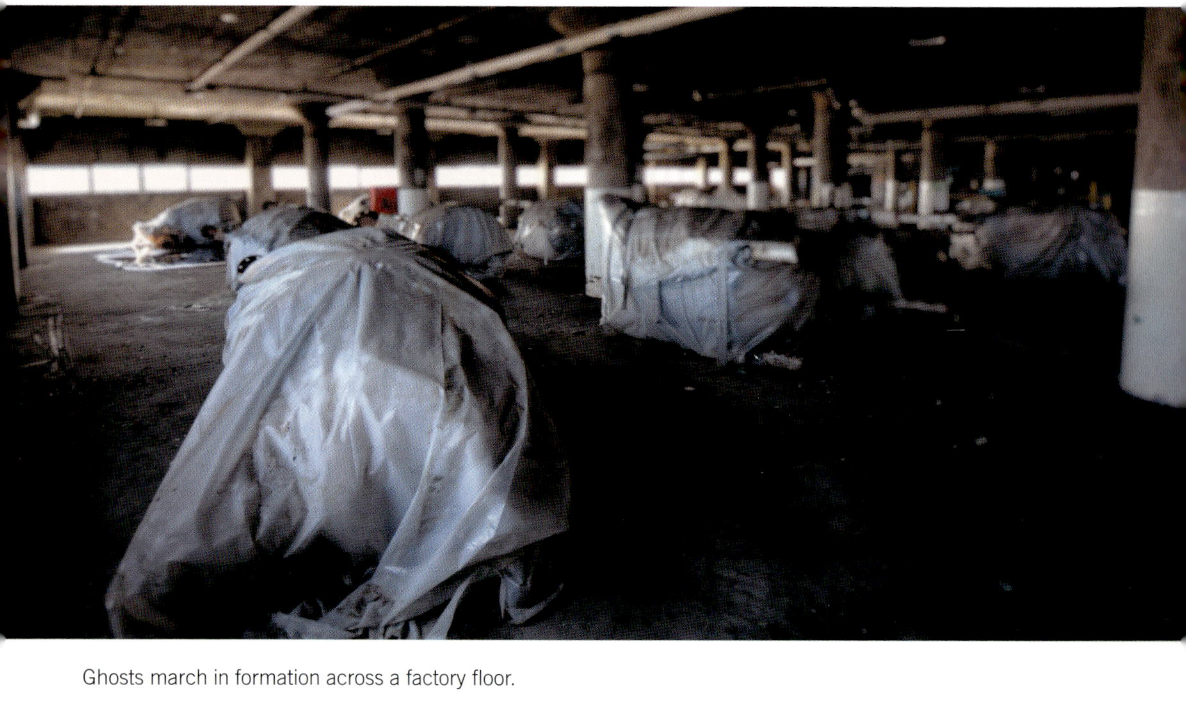

Ghosts march in formation across a factory floor.

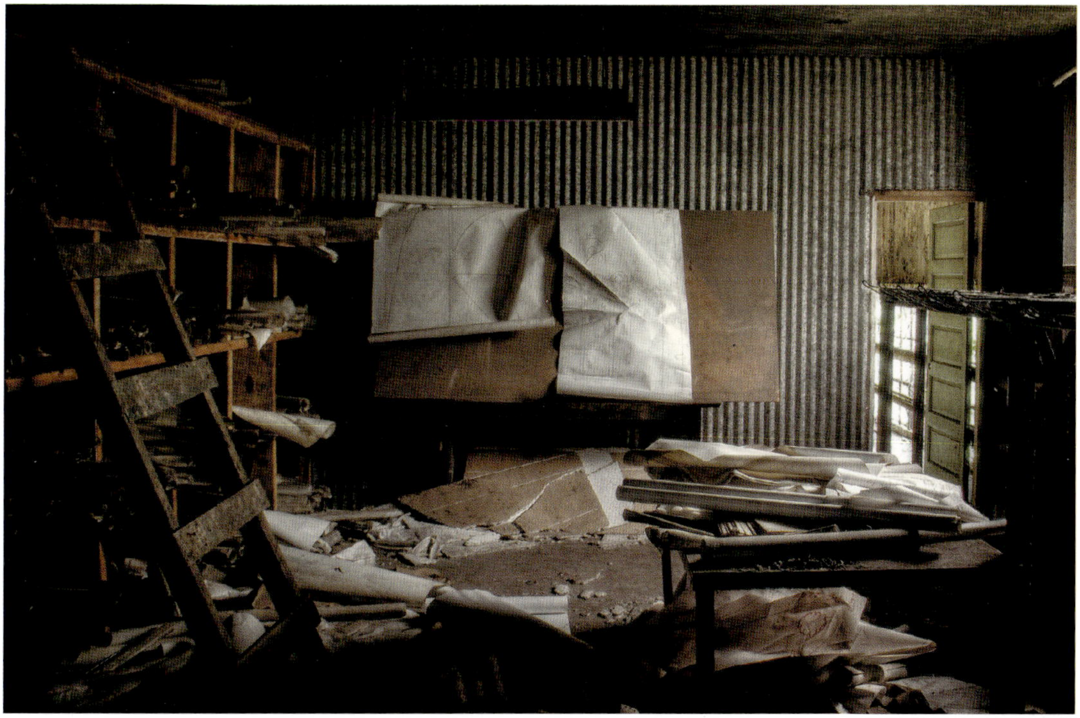

Eldritch scrolls proffer their arcane schematics.

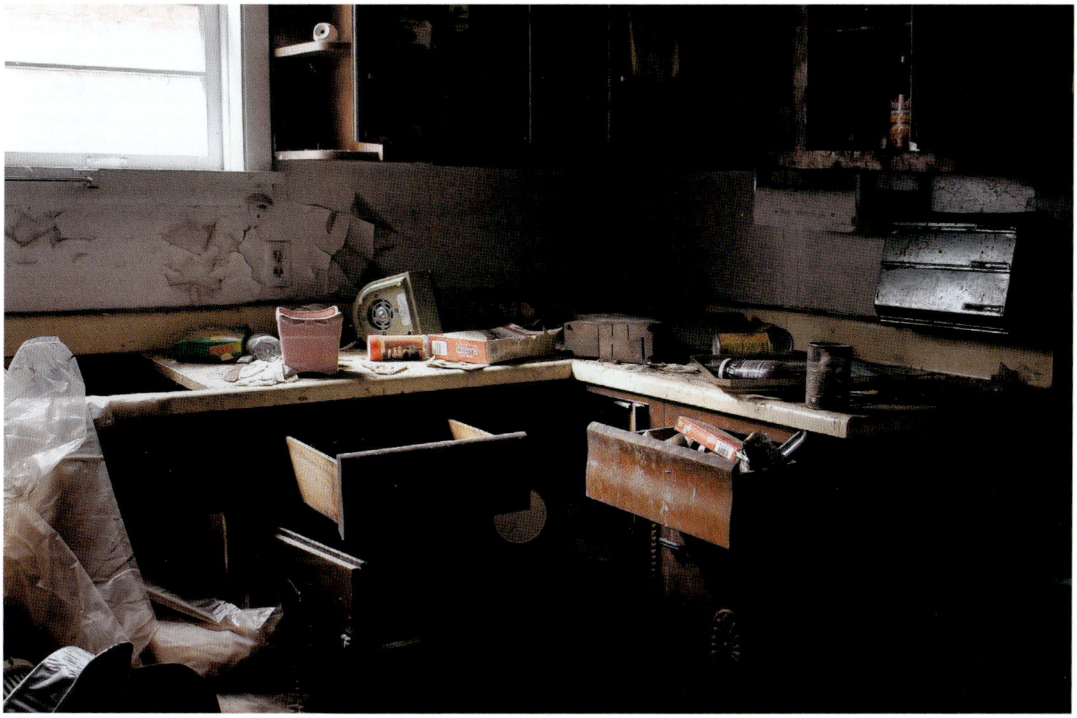

The remains of a life, seen in a Gary kitchen.

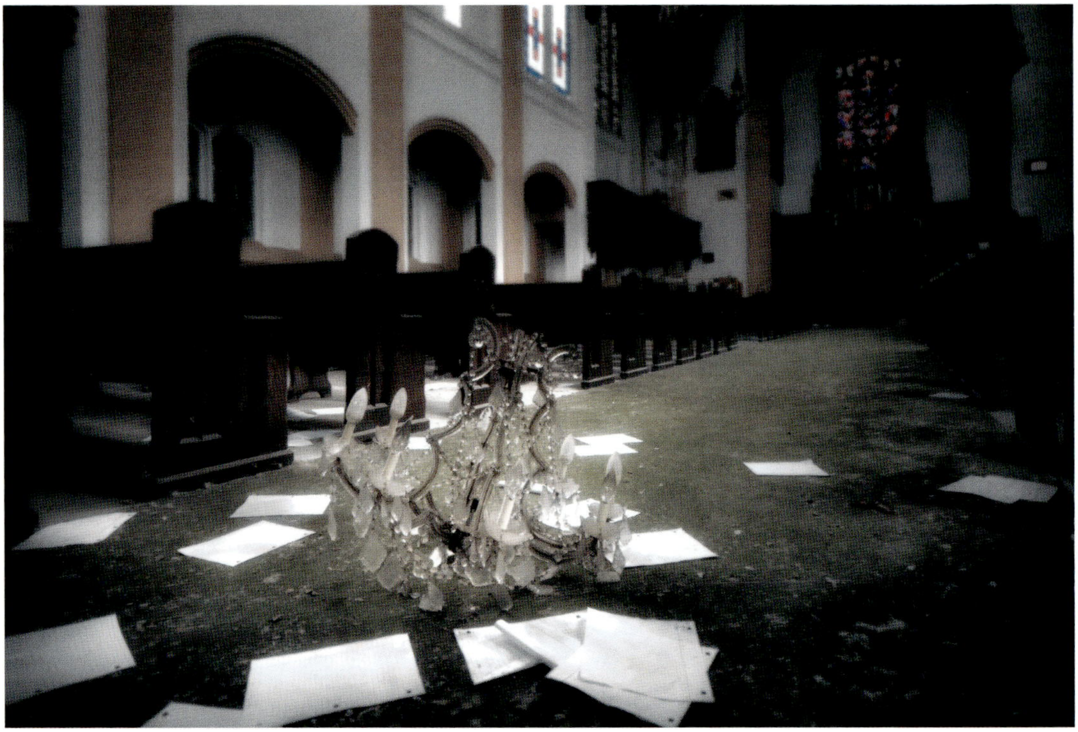

A chandelier poses rakishly in the aisle of a Chicago church.

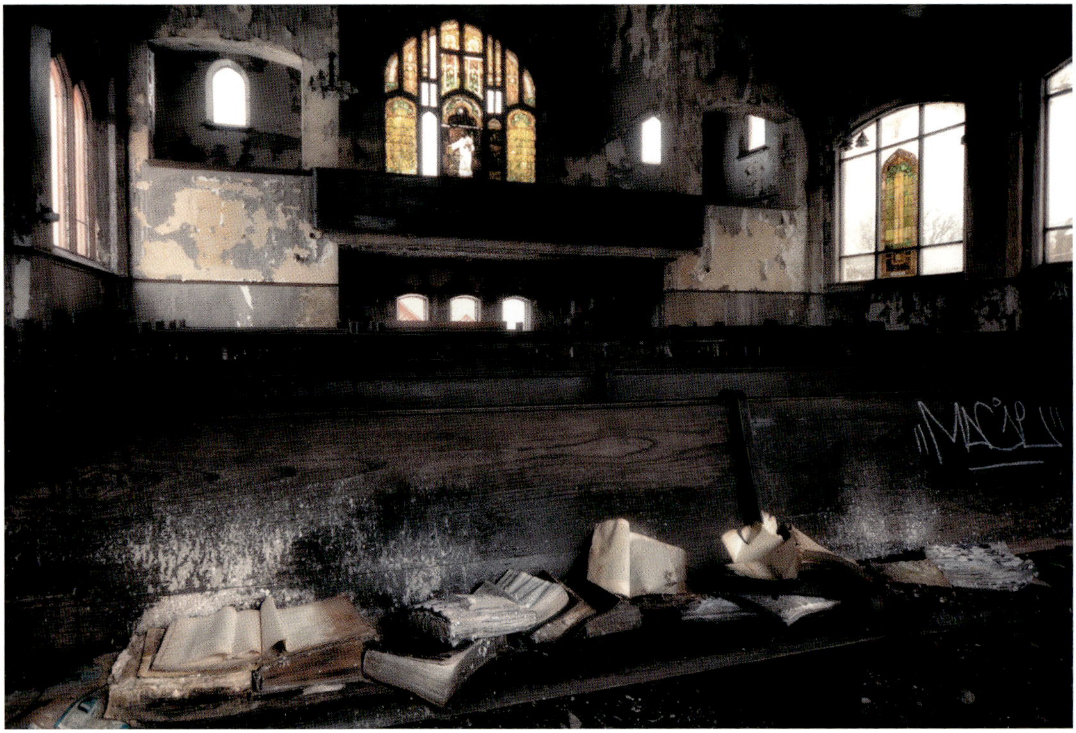

Have you heard the good news?

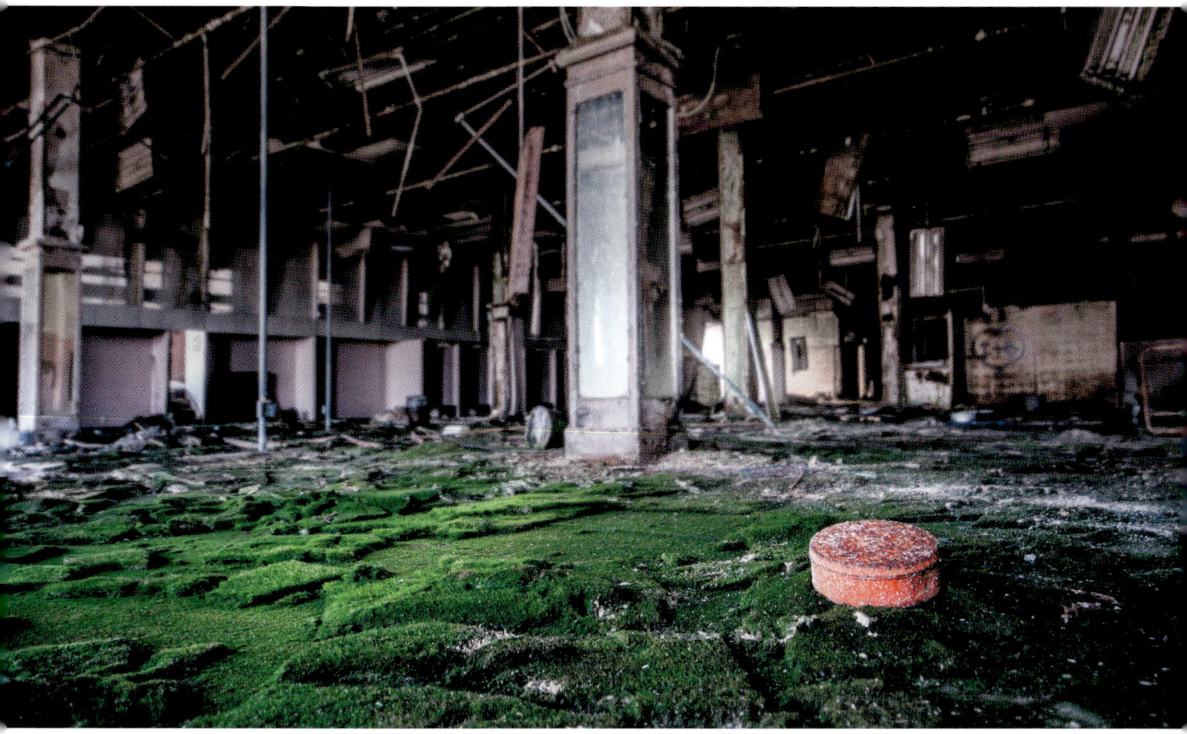

Moss carpeting an abandoned department store.

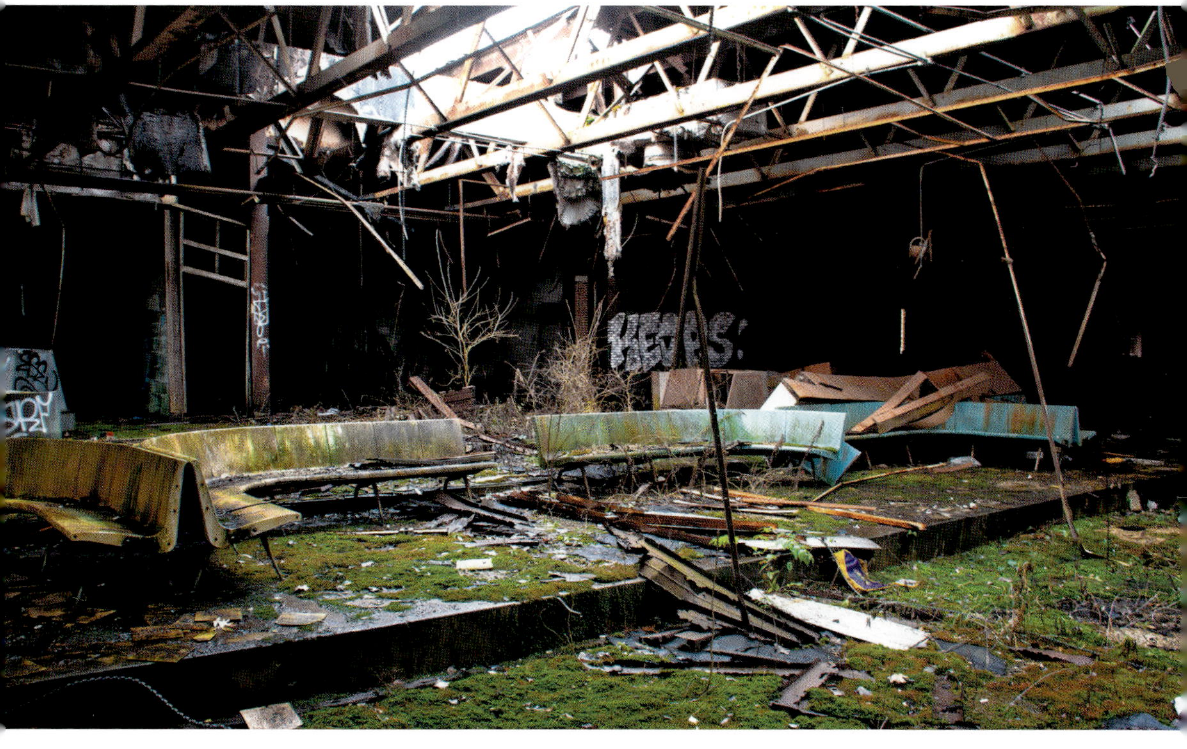

This building was so stripped down and rotted that it took a while to identify it as a bowling alley.

6

TRUTH, HONESTY, AND OTHER BULLSHIT

Photography has been beset by questions of authenticity almost since its inception. The medium's presumed veracity was at odds with the ease with which pictures could be doctored, altered, or through techniques such as photomontage or double exposure, staged outright. When a genre often showcases the pathos and desolation of old and derelict places, it is appropriate to wonder how "real" they are, and what that even means. Urbex photography has addressed these issues in its own, at times appropriately rogue, ways.

Broadly speaking, the attitudes run along a spectrum. One end can be described as "take only photos, leave only footprints," with a focus on preserving found sites in the way nature conservancies might, and shooting them just as they find them. The underlying philosophy might be described as documentarian, with an emphasis on minimally processing the finished images, whether through Photoshop or other ways. The motto on the other end could be "the ends justify the means." These might be the explorers that rearrange the objects they shoot or bring their own props to insert into the shot. They may blur the line between explorers and vandals by trashing the places they shoot if they are deemed to appear not abandoned enough. The same attitudes apply to the finished images, though usually with the goal of creating the most "goth" picture possible (think: doom and despair). Admittedly, few explorers are entirely on this extreme end, but they are out there. Most, however, fall somewhere in the middle, shading towards the documentary-minded side. If literal truthfulness is the goal, then it is pretty clear which side is in the right. Having briefly outlined the general attitudes of the urbex community, I thought it made sense to discuss my own, if only to show the interested reader the ideals that informed the creation of these photographs.

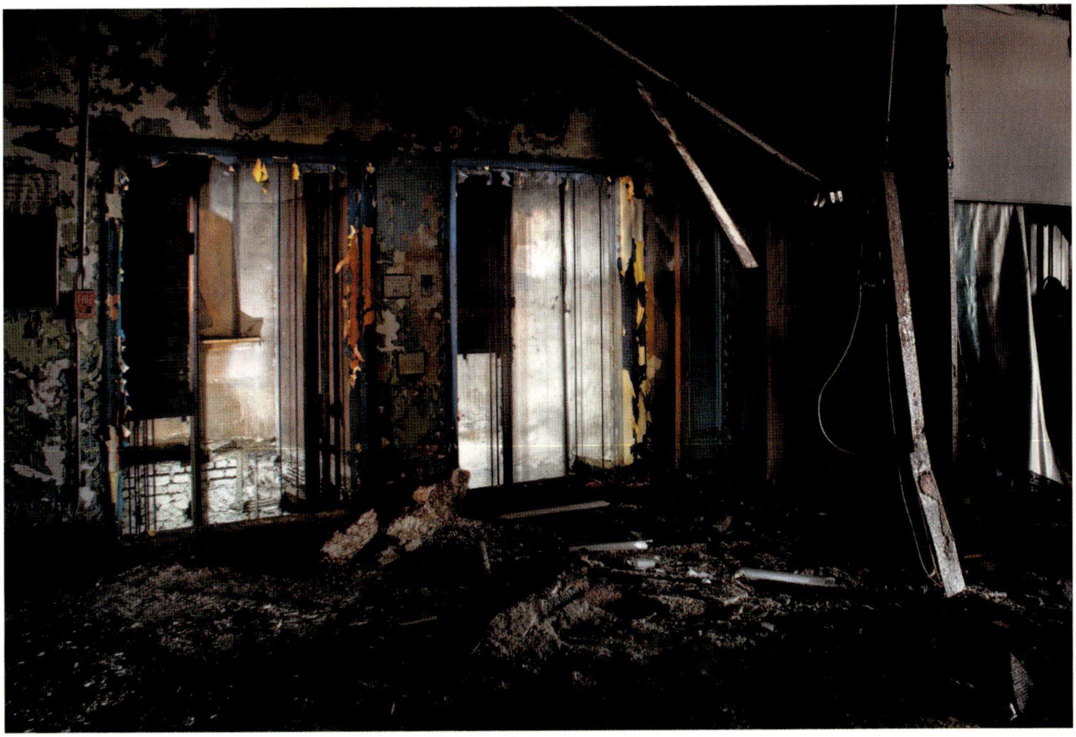

Surely a spectral glow does not come from the elevators?

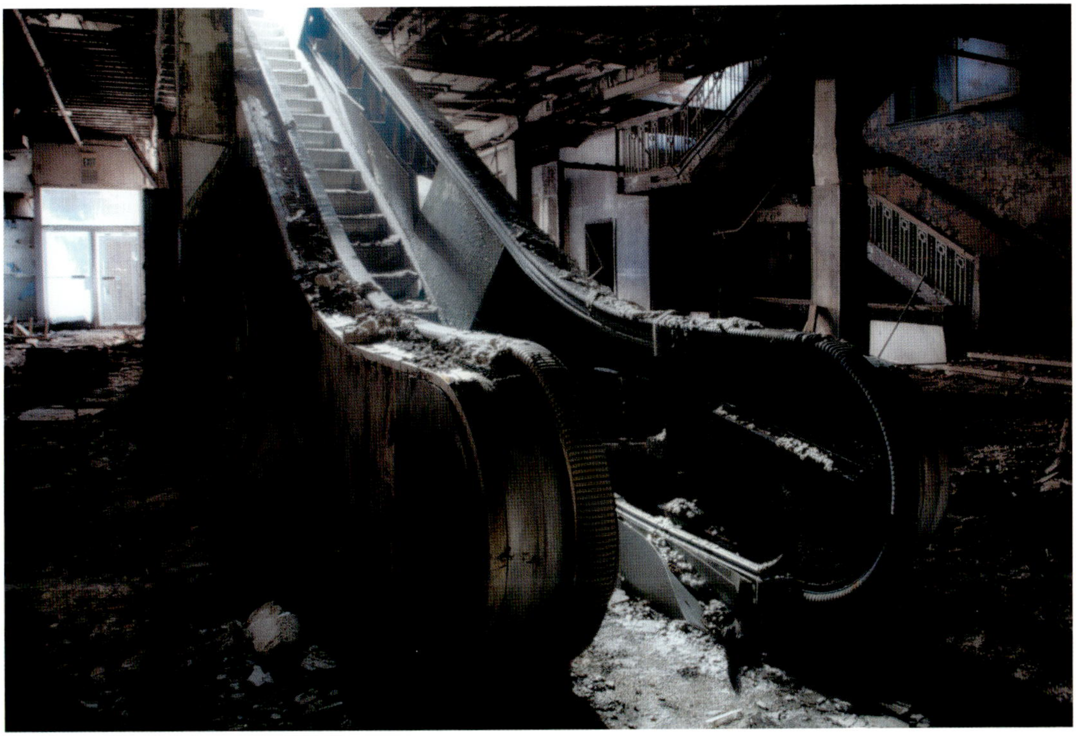

Is heaven an escalator ride away, or be that a trick of the light?

I tend to be less sentimental or protective of the derelict places and things I photograph than many other explorers I know. The reasons for this are as I laid out already: I see abandonment and subsequent decay as the process that allows me to do what I do. Overly bemoaning a beloved building's demise at, say, the business end of a bulldozer, arson, or collapse, is akin to biting the hand that feeds. This attitude does not preclude my respect for these places nor my desire for them to last as long as possible, so I adhere to the general rule to not publicly disclose names and locations of places, unless they are already public knowledge. Likewise, bringing things to insert into a scene, rearranging objects or further destroying them in order to further some aesthetic is off base, as it inserts unneeded artifice and hastens the demise of these old places. However, I find taking an occasional souvenir perfectly acceptable, especially in cases where there is clearly no chance a building will be rehabbed or repurposed. To illustrate just how often these occasions come along, in over a decade of dedicated exploration I've taken exactly two things from abandoned buildings: a large tin of cold-war era survival crackers, issued by the old U.S. Civil Defense in case of nuclear war and one of thousands moldering in an old school attic, and an intact piece of stained-glass window, from a church on the demolition block.

As far as photoshopping or otherwise editing photos, my starting point is that of attempting to create art. Subjectively, this means getting across in the finished photos the grandeur, beauty, desolation, or otherworldliness that I experienced in the places I've shot. These emotions do not have to be made up, as these places are truly affecting (if they're not already, why photograph them?), but capturing these feelings effectively can be tricky. The reason for this has to do with the nature of urbex photography, which often requires shooting in very dark or cramped spaces, or where lighting is very uneven. Overcoming these challenges can often be done on the spot using various lenses or exposure times, or by lighting the subject yourself. However, various kinds of post-processing may be necessary, from adjusting the tones and colors to cropping or moving the image. Finally, techniques such as stacking or using high dynamic range programs (HDR for short) may be helpful, though this is where issues of authenticity start to crop up.

These last two methods can even out an image that contains both very dark and bright areas. Think of taking a snapshot of a room with a window during a sunny day. The bright light coming through the window will likely be much stronger than whatever artificial light is on in the room. A single photo can either show the room and have the window be a blinding white glare or show the view outside while leaving the room almost pitch black. Stacking or HDR will use a series of images that are identical except for differing exposures and combine the "hot' and "cold" spots to create a more balanced image.

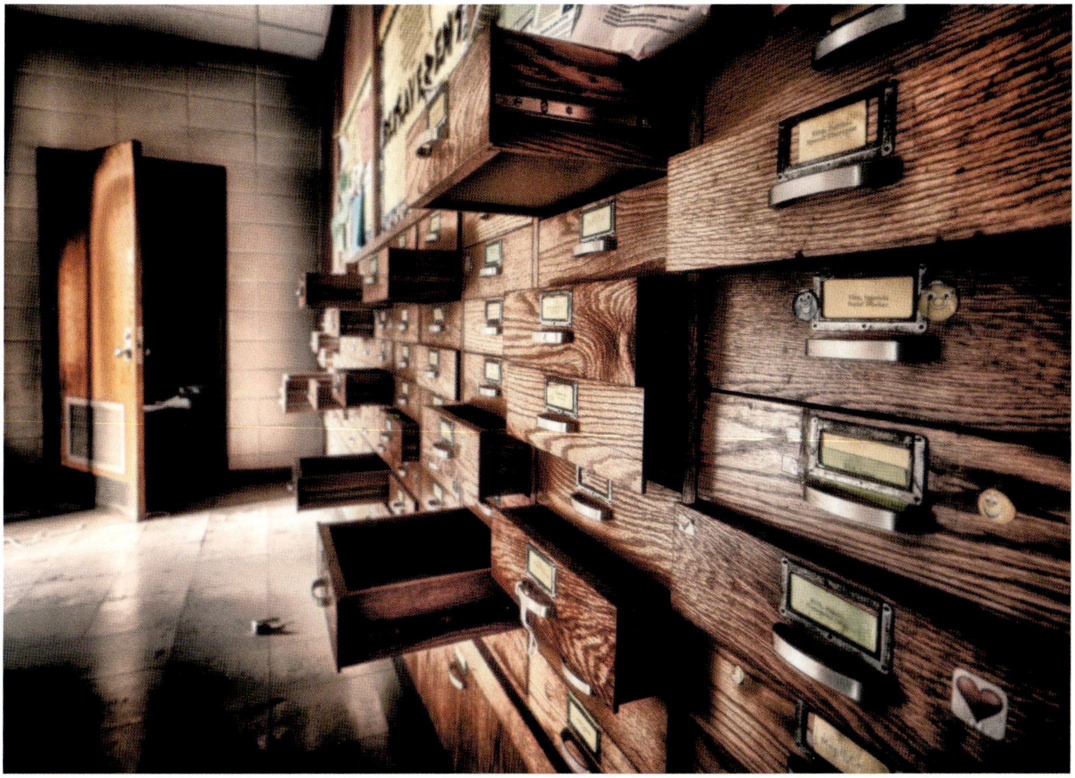

HDR processing with strong contrast.

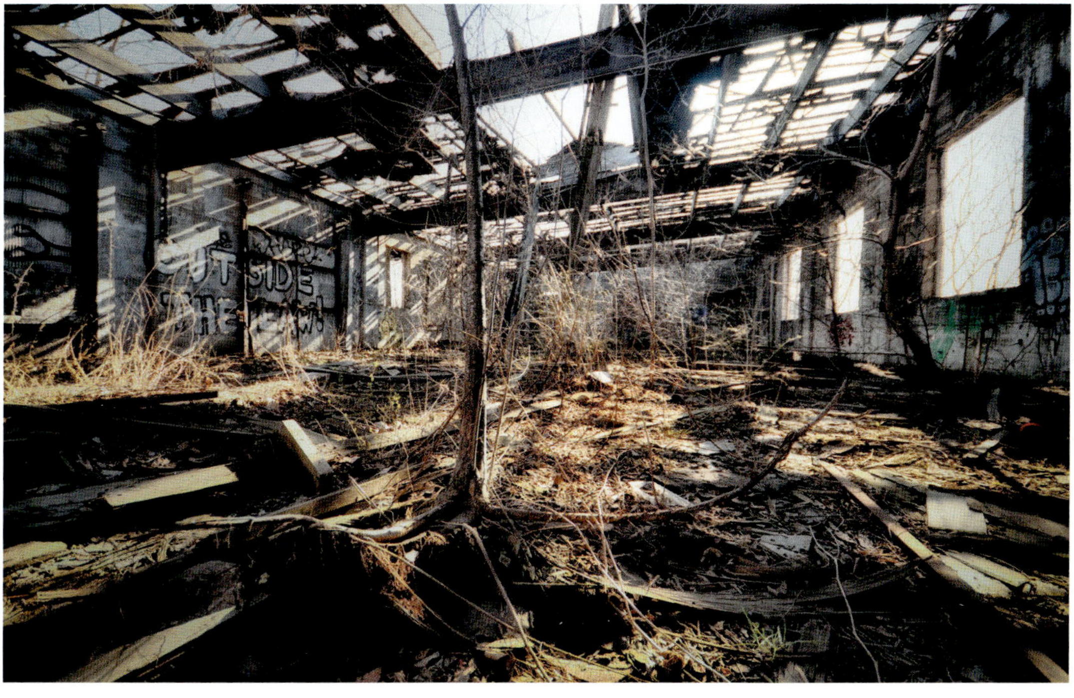

HDR processing to even out bright sky with shadowed interior.

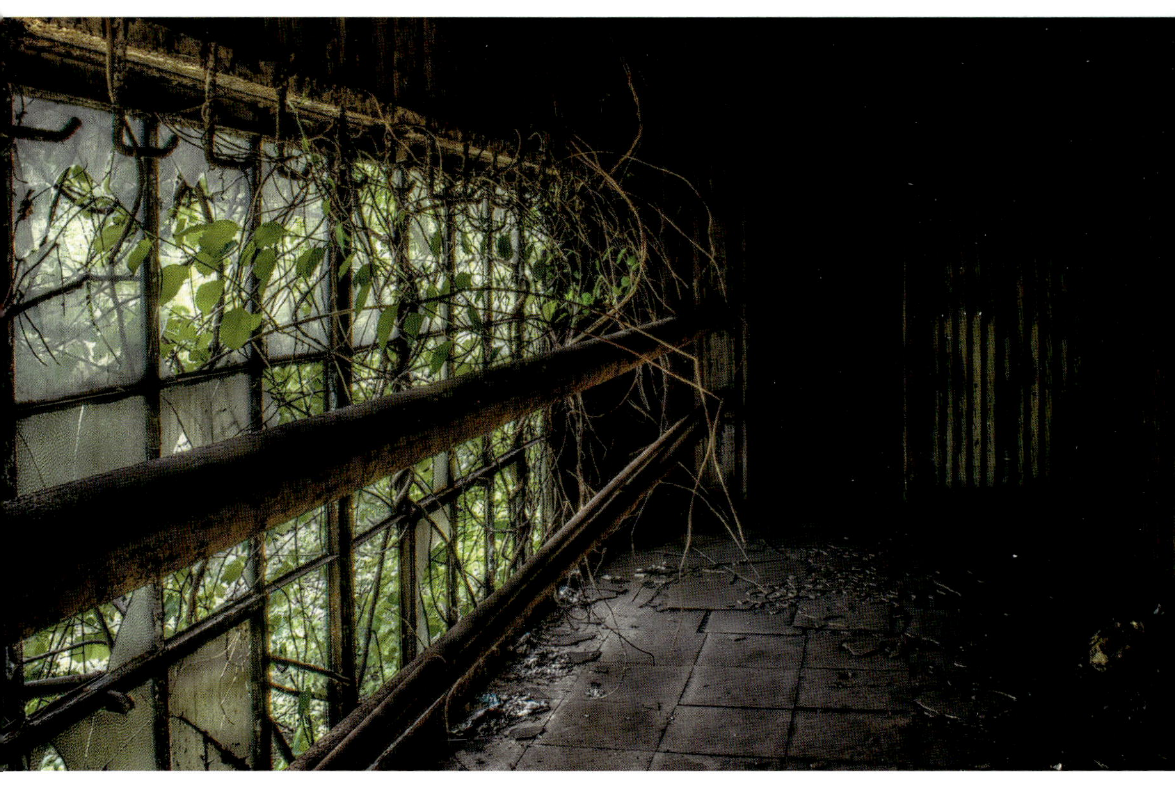

HDR processing to bring out details in the dark.

If overdone, this can create images that look fake or unnatural. The lighting can be too balanced, making the overall picture appear flat, or the colors can turn garish and look more like a cartoon than a photograph. But if done well, the effect actually simulates how we see the world. The human eye adjusts quickly as we look from brighter to darker areas around us, leaving the impression that the light in our environment is much more balanced than it actually is. Thus, some heavily processed photos can be a more accurate representation of how a scene looks to us than any single snapshot can.

What this means is that any processing or alteration does not necessarily take away from the veracity of the end photo. Rather, they are options that allow for creative and artistic expression by drawing attention either towards or away from various aspects or parts of the image. And as art is subjective, these choices are valid so long as they create a work that is affecting and somehow resonates with the viewer. The answer as to whether a picture is honest can be summed up by repurposing a quote on how to recognize pornography by former Supreme Court Justice Potter Stewart: "I know it when I see it."

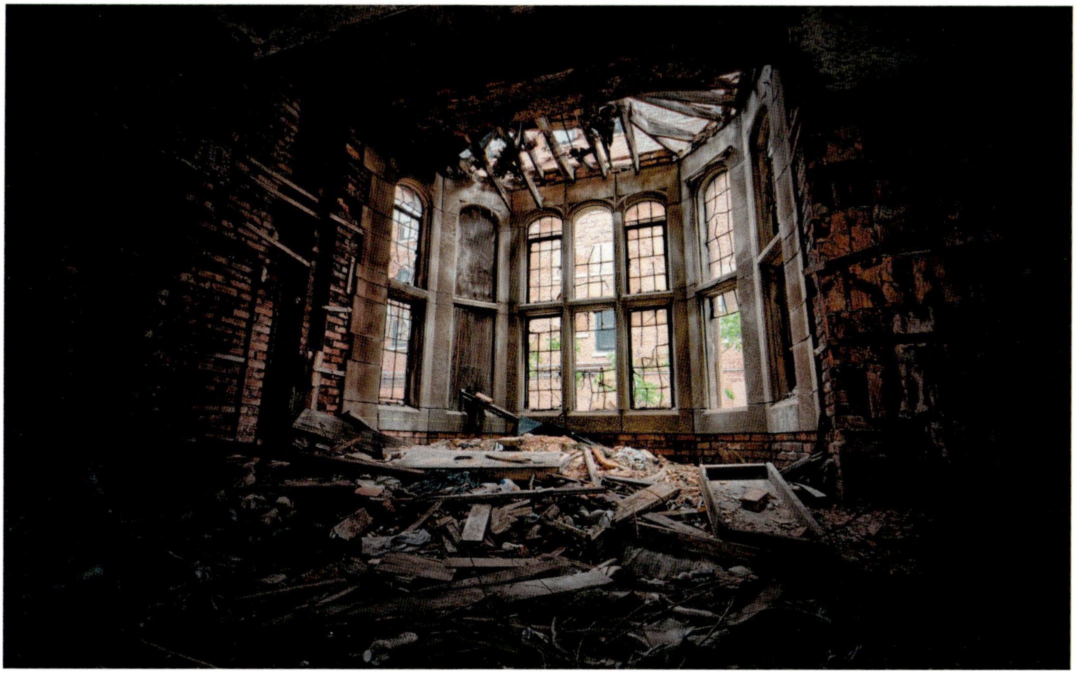

HDR processing for a painting-like look.

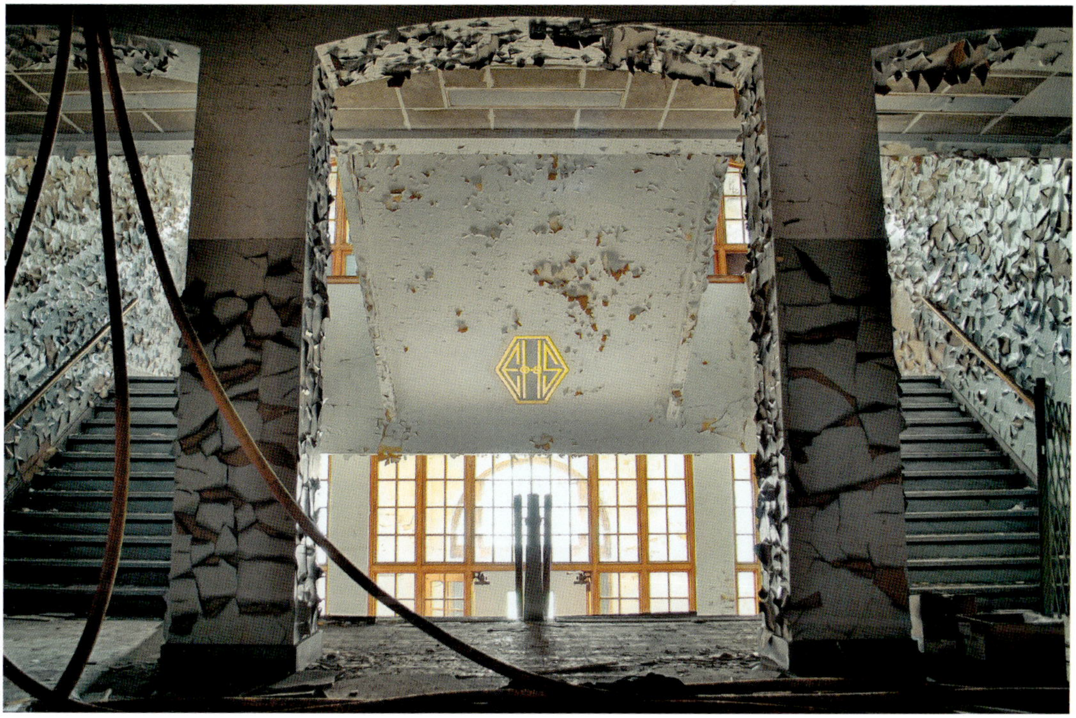

HDR processing can do wonders for textures like this peeling paint.

7

OH, THE PLACES YOU'LL GO!

One of urban exploration's many charms is that the explorer gets to visit places that would normally have been barred to them during their lifetimes. There can be a slight thrill in getting to see some things up close and at one's leisure, even if those things have fallen into ruin. The feeling of being the last person on earth, not uncommon during urban explorations, can be especially strong in these off-limit places. They can range from the rather prosaic, like quiet little back rooms and offices, to the monstrous halls of heavy industry. In this first case, it's the gloriously kitschy bathroom of a home untenanted for the last three decades.

Here are the various conference rooms and storage areas hiding at the end of dark high school hallways, along with a cushy waiting room to a pastor's office, complete with stained glass arched windows.

A special case is the attic of a particular high school. It seems to have been a storage area for books and equipment, but at some point also became the place students would sneak into in order to scrawl their names and graduating years on the timber walls and ceilings. The oldest inscription I could find was from the 1930s, with the predominance coming from the sixties onward. They turned the entire attic into a colorful fresco. These signatures were challenging to photograph in the near darkness of the place, requiring using flashlights angled just so in order to adequately light the shots without too many deep shadows or harsh glare.

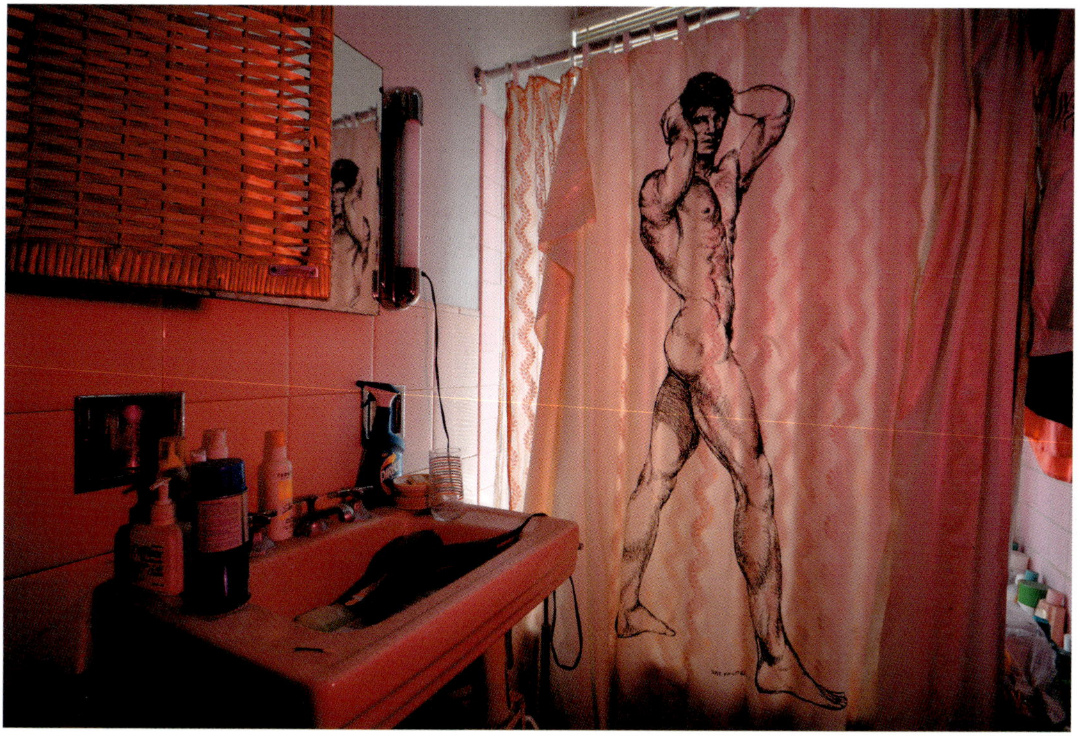

Hey sugar, can you get my back?

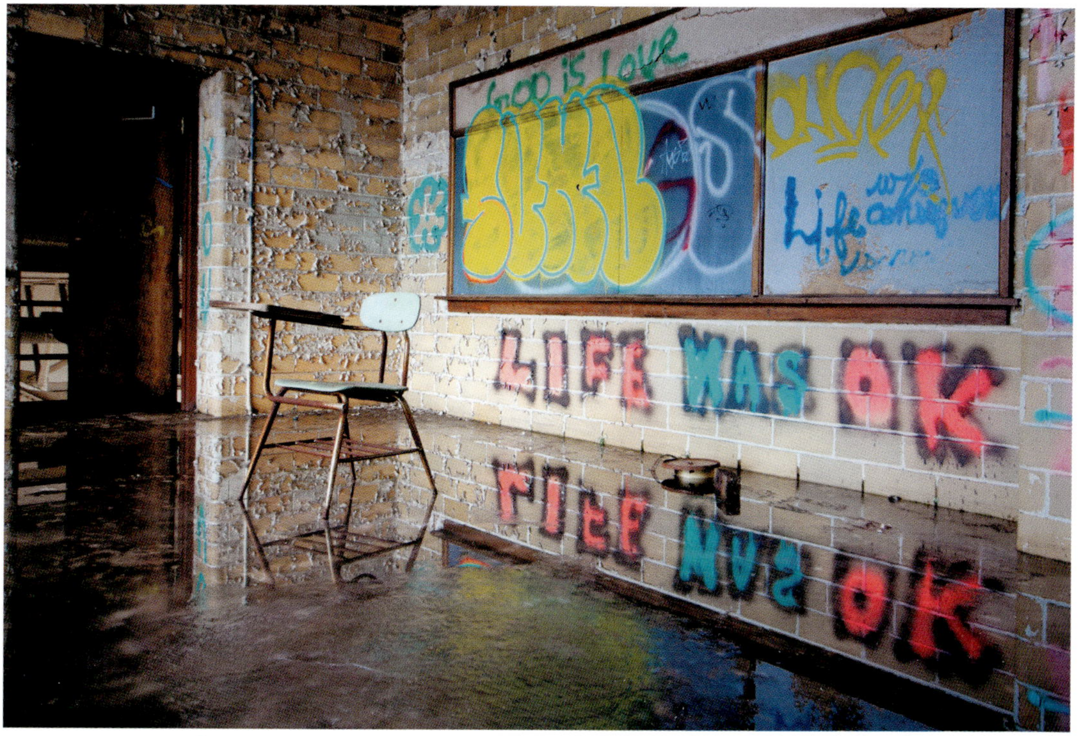

Taggers, on average, are a more optimist cohort than urbexers.

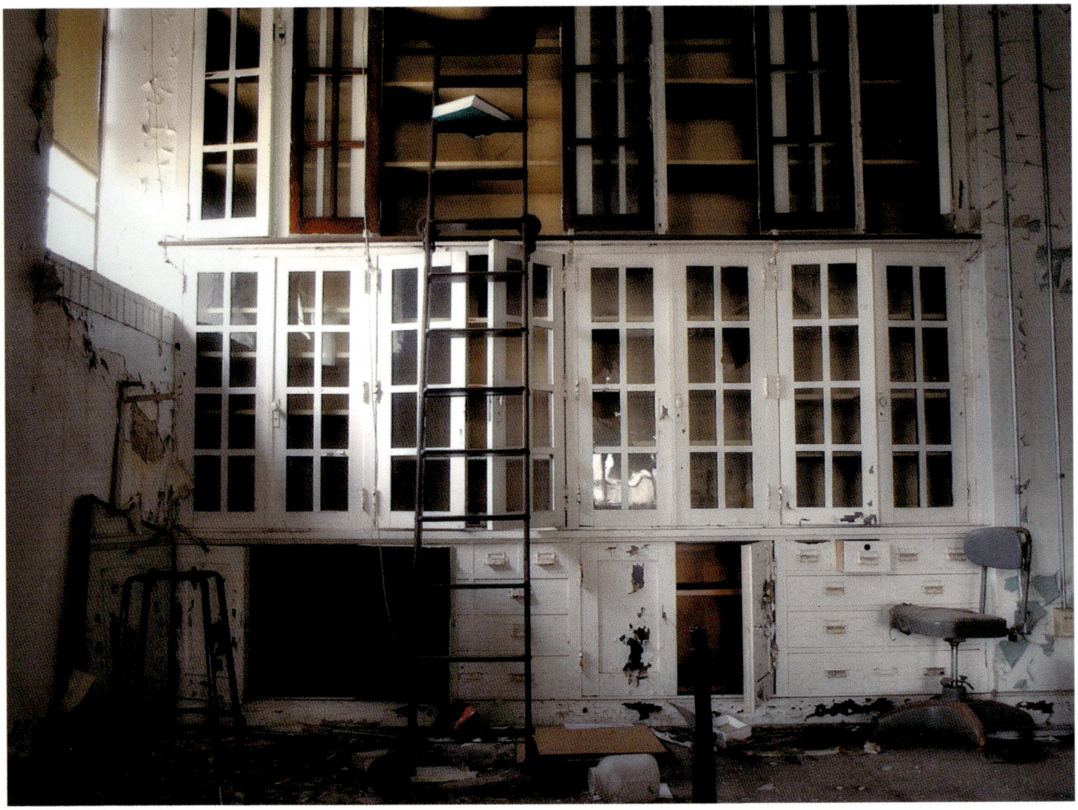

The ladder goes to eleven.

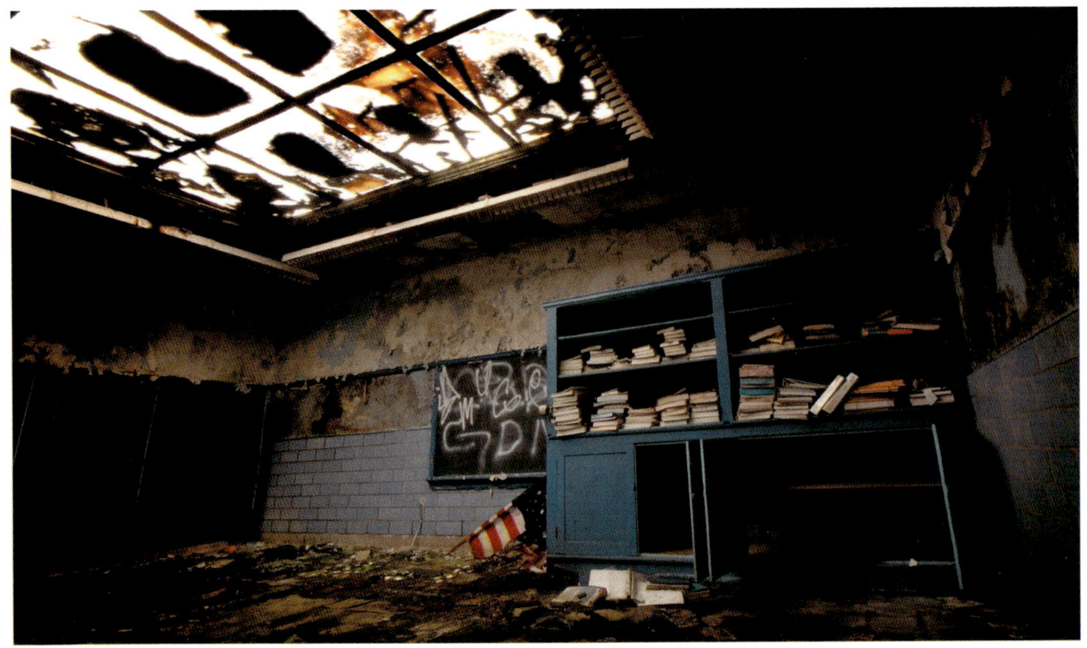

Skylight looks over a bookshelf with flag.

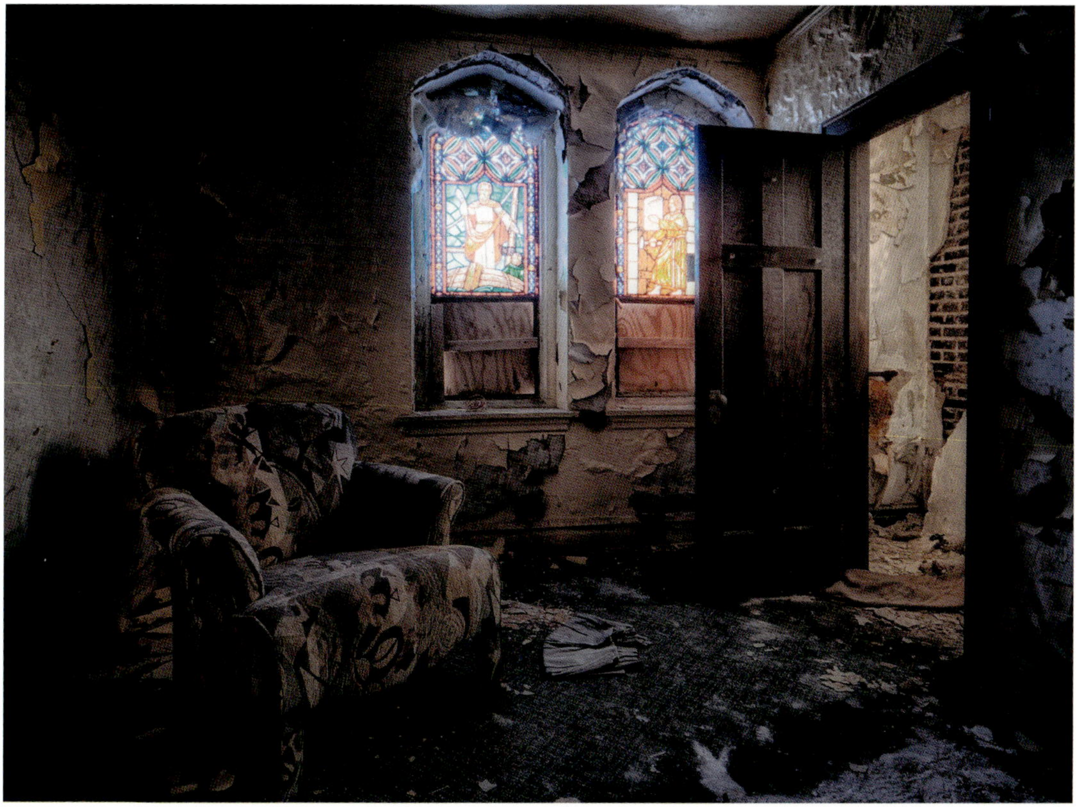

Wait here until the pastor calls you in.

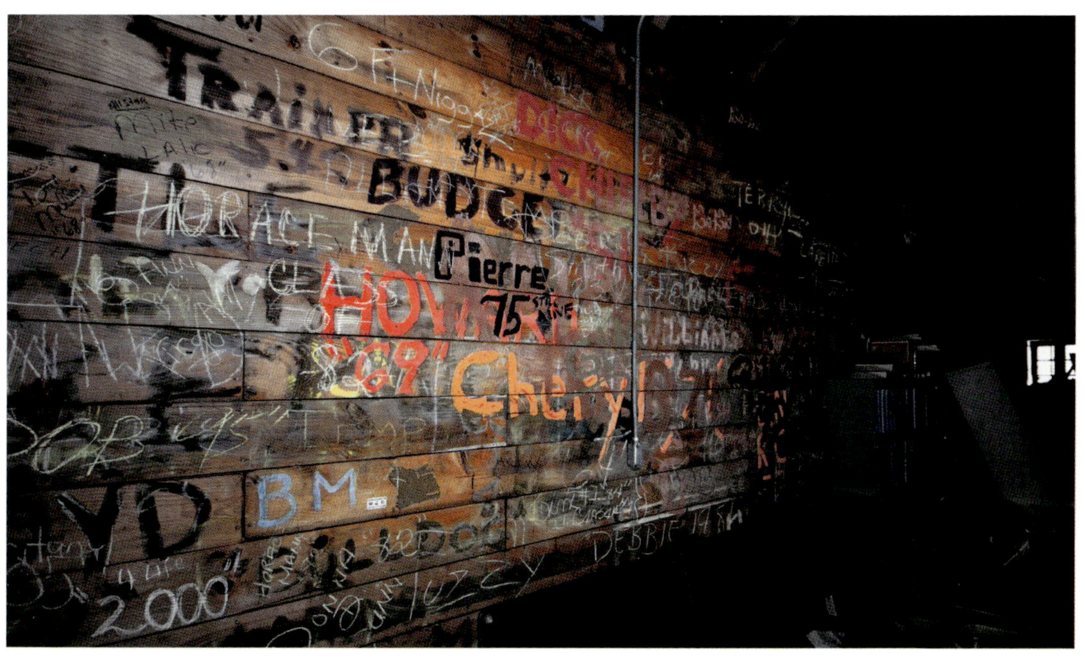

I was here 1.

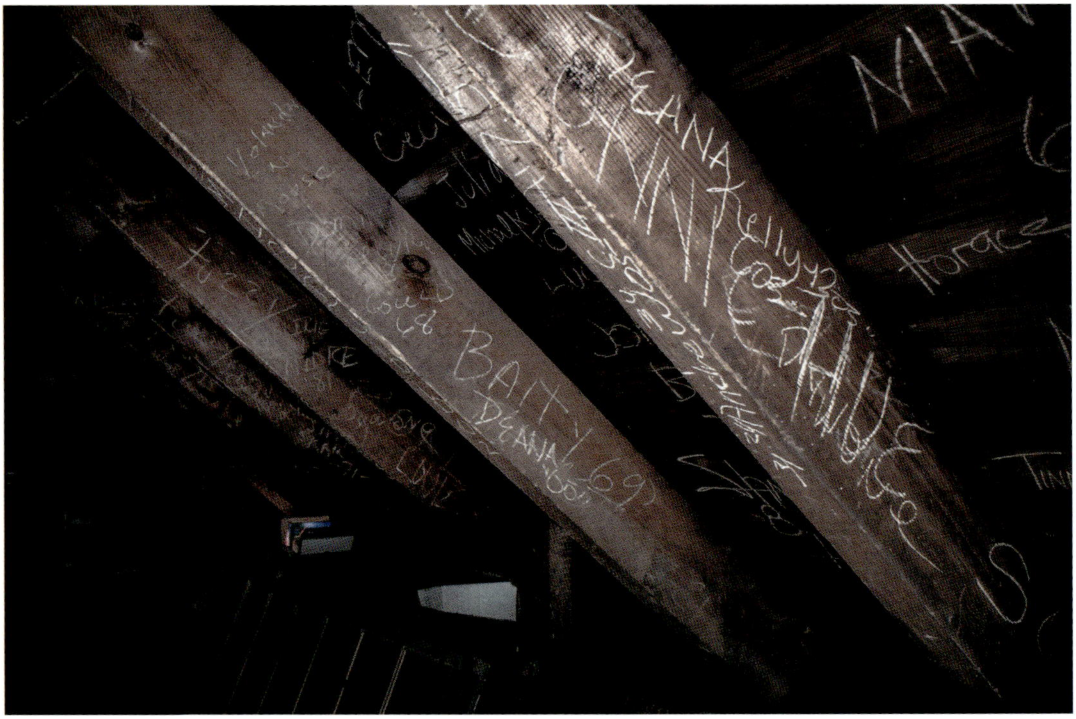

I was here 2.

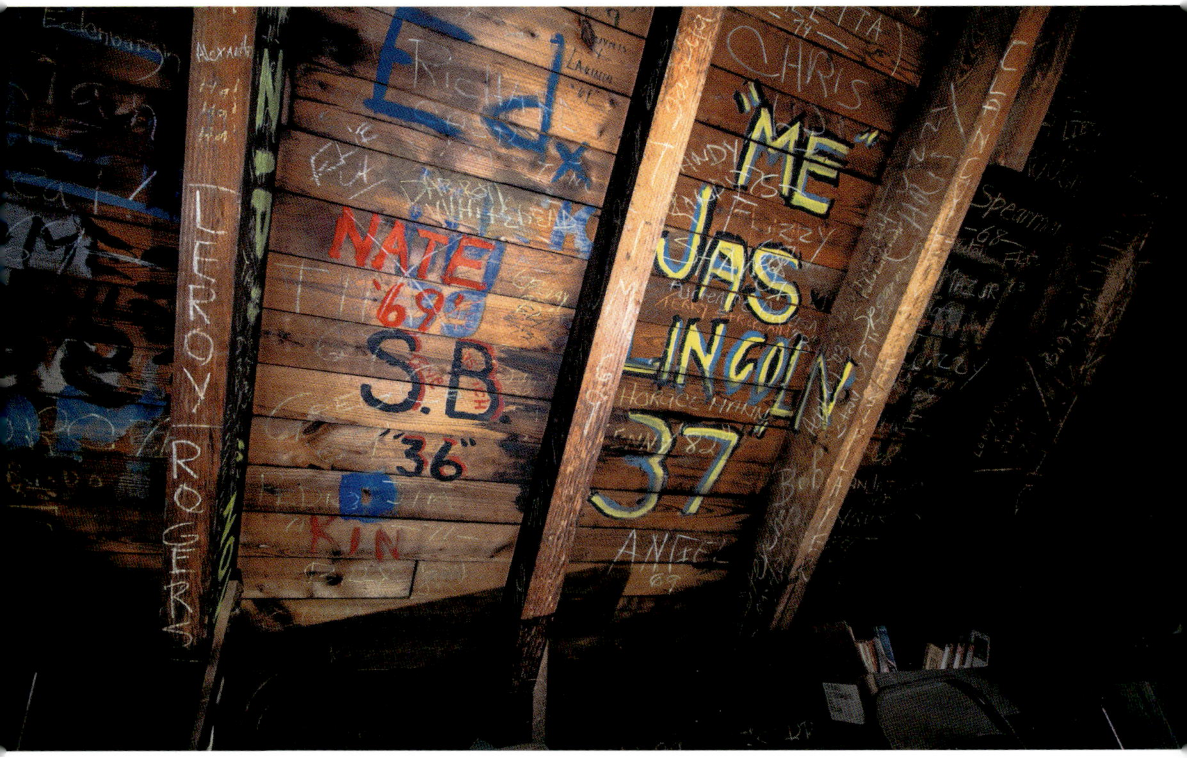

I was here 3.

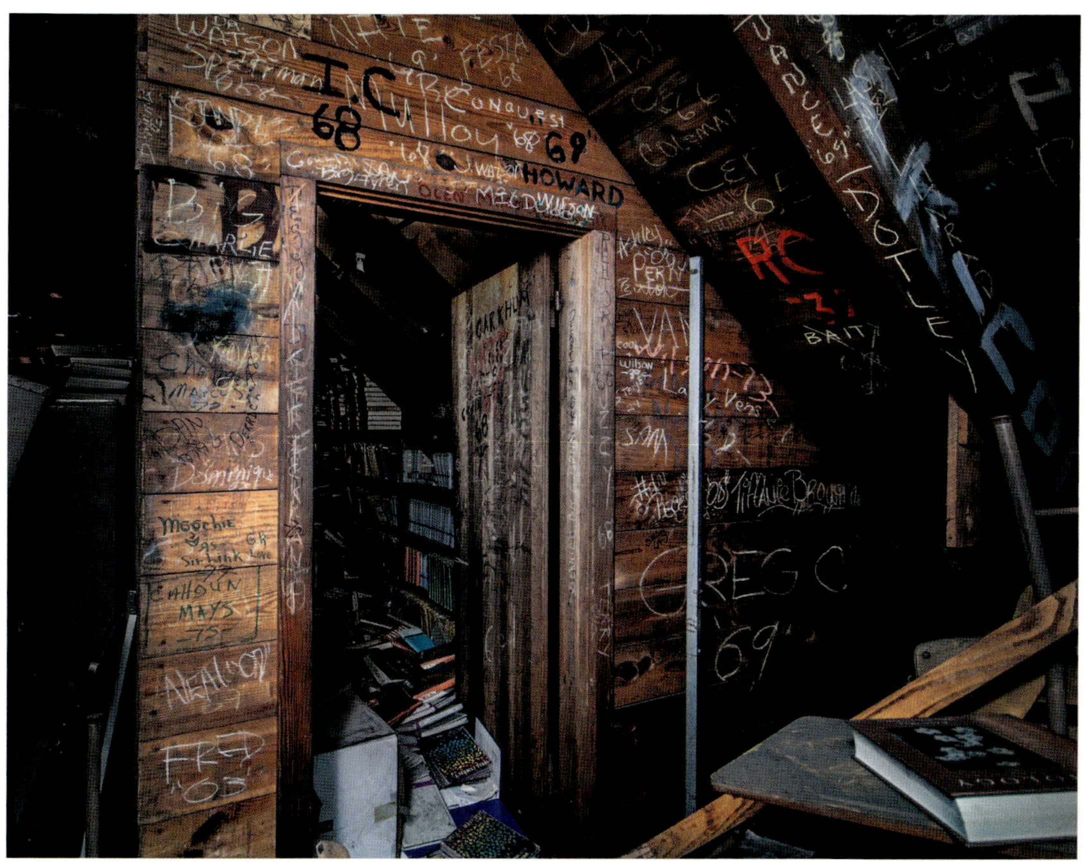

I was here 4.

Until recently, in south suburban Riverdale stood a massive poultry feed mill next to the railroad tracks. Disused since the mid-seventies, it was a thirteen-story behemoth of rebar and rust. It was one of the places my friends and I cut our teeth on when we first started exploring, before we had even heard the term "urban exploration." The floors everywhere were shot through with holes, both from design and decay, and filled with the remains of conveyors, conduits, and machinery. Regardless of material, all had at least a tinge of the same ruddy hue from the rust everywhere. In the summer, the dark, concrete interior was always appreciably cooler than the outside, making it a welcoming spot during sweltering August days. However, in the winter cold, winds would whip through the edifice, especially on the higher floors, and discourage all but the hardiest souls from staying too long. Those intent on getting to the roof had to brave some truly rickety stairs as well as a dodgy skybridge, to be ultimately rewarded by breathtaking views of … well, nothing, really. You could easily see the skyline of Chicago almost twenty miles north, but it wasn't enough to reward the risk. Luckily, rooftops are their own reward.

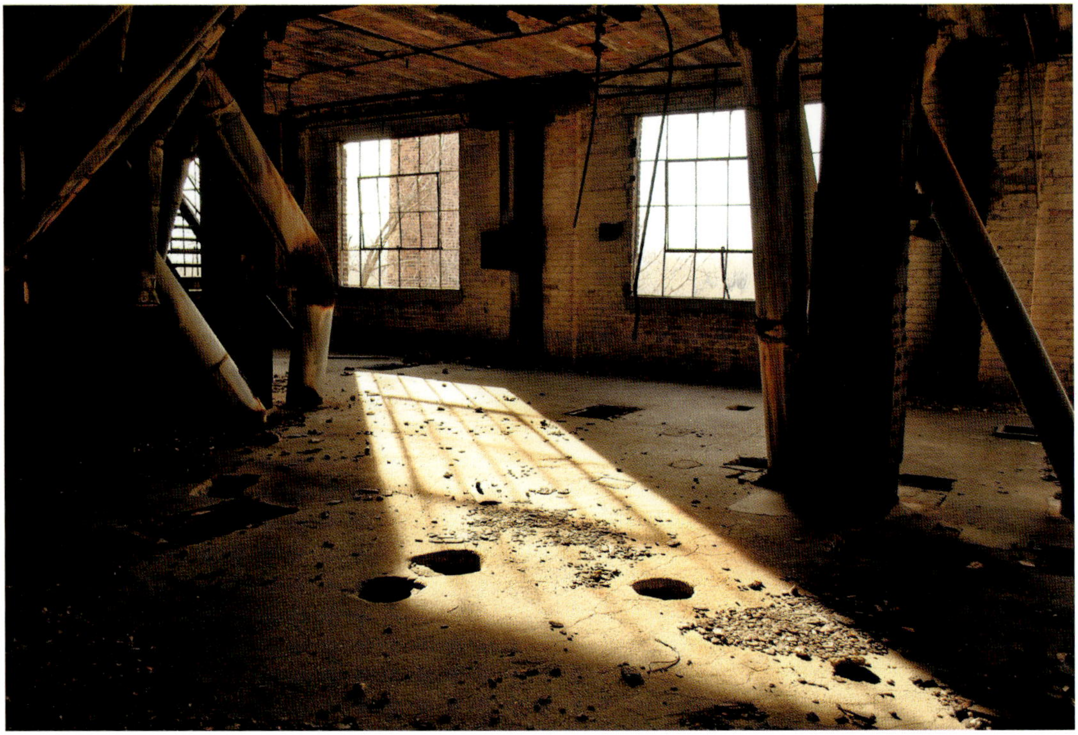

Morning light creates a sundial on a factory floor.

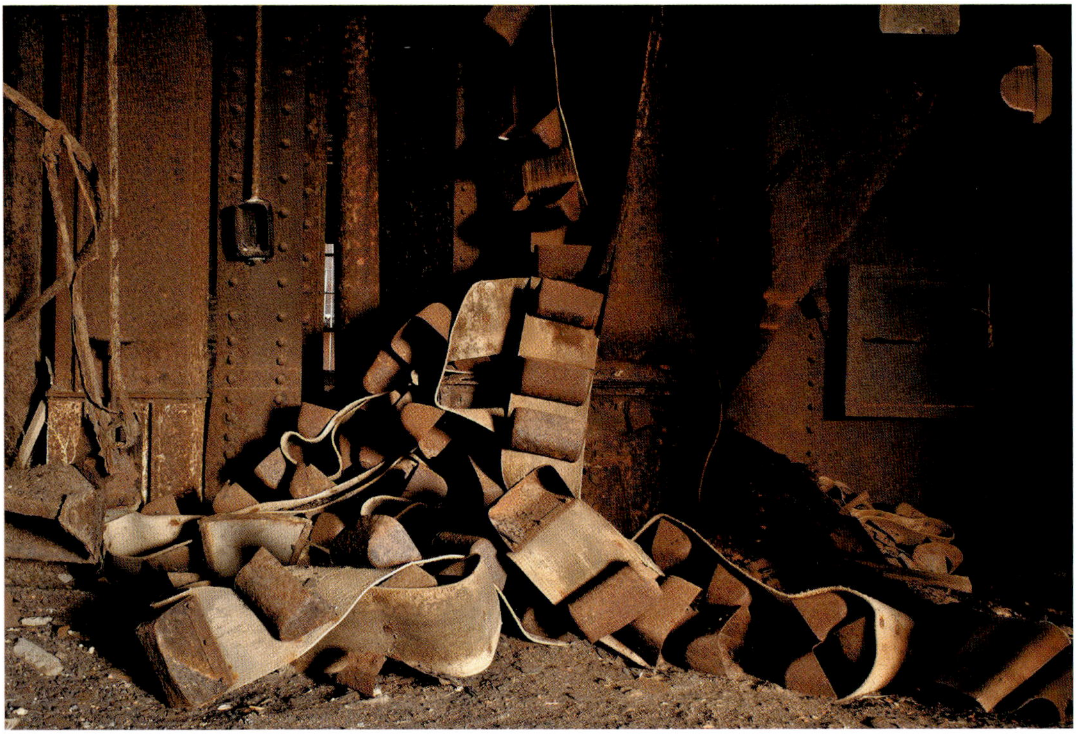

The granary conveyor belt performs its impression of an 80s cassette tape.

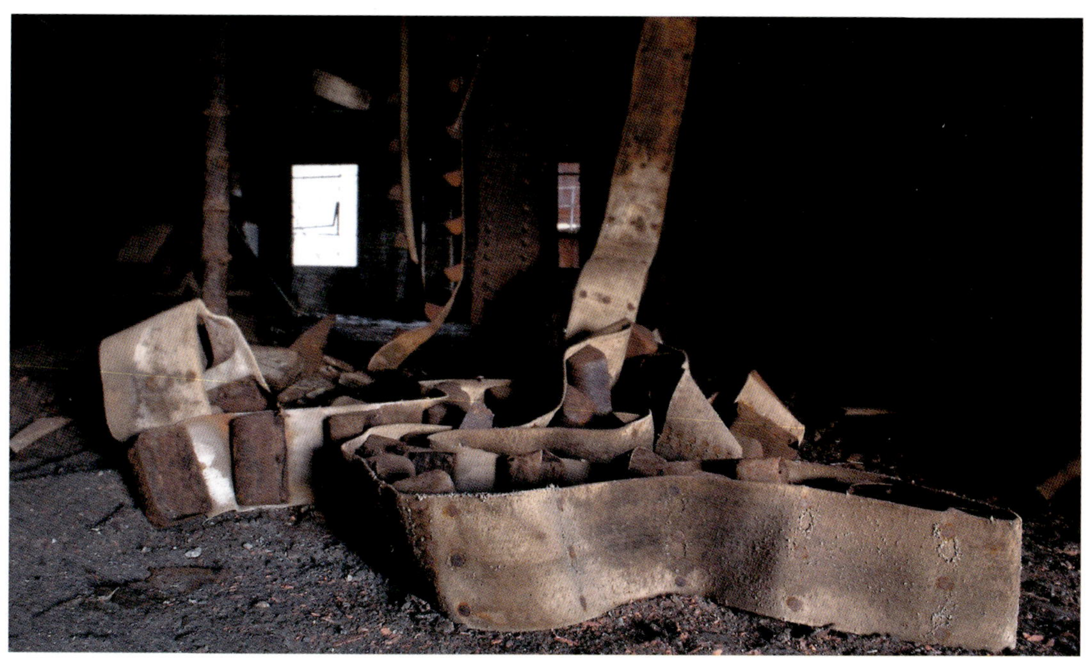

Belts spill forth.

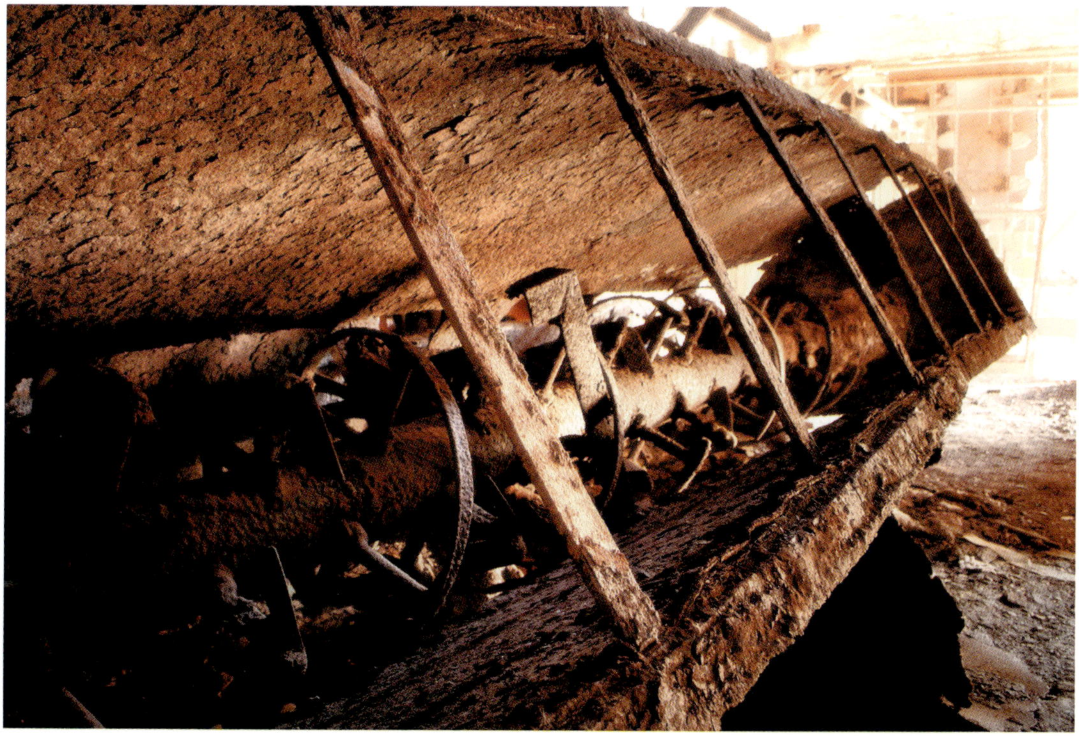

Machinery rusts on the floor of the feed plant.

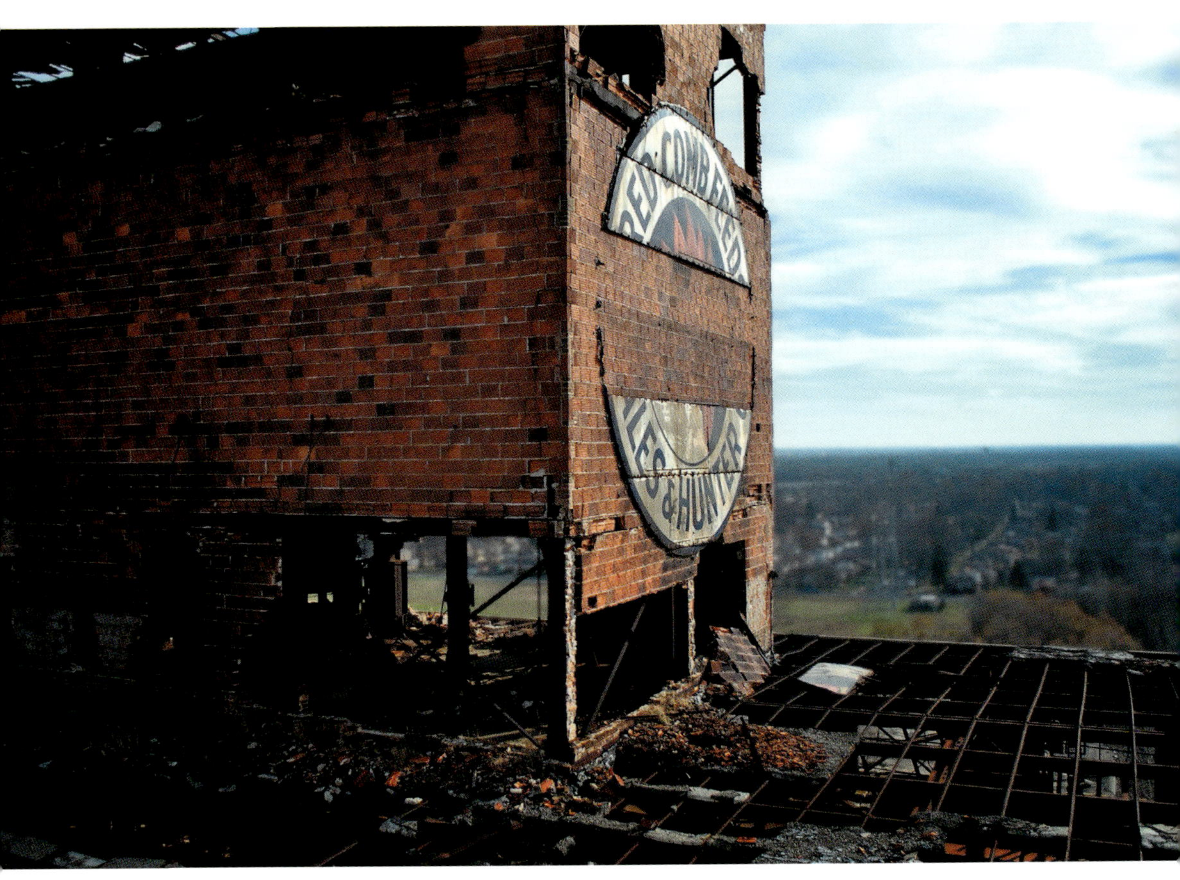

Behold the lands of southern Cook County!

Hospitals, for obvious reasons, aren't places most people are keen to visit while they are in operation. Once derelict, they can have quite a lot to see for an explorer. Very expensive equipment winds up staying behind, possibly because it can be too expensive to move, out of date, or actually built into the hospital itself. This was the case with a famous Chicago hospital, whose facade once was featured in the opening credits of a nineties-era medical procedural television drama. When it closed, it was because a new, modern facility was built next door to replace the century-old original, and most equipment was removed. But to my delight, things like operating rooms and radiology equipment were all left behind. It also had a grand surgical theater on the penthouse level, which featured large skylights (since painted over) which may have provided better lighting than the early incandescent bulbs. Another hospital on the north side of the city had a hyperbaric chamber, big enough to accommodate a wheelchair. These were chances to view these places up close, without the benefit of years of medical schooling or a debilitating illness.

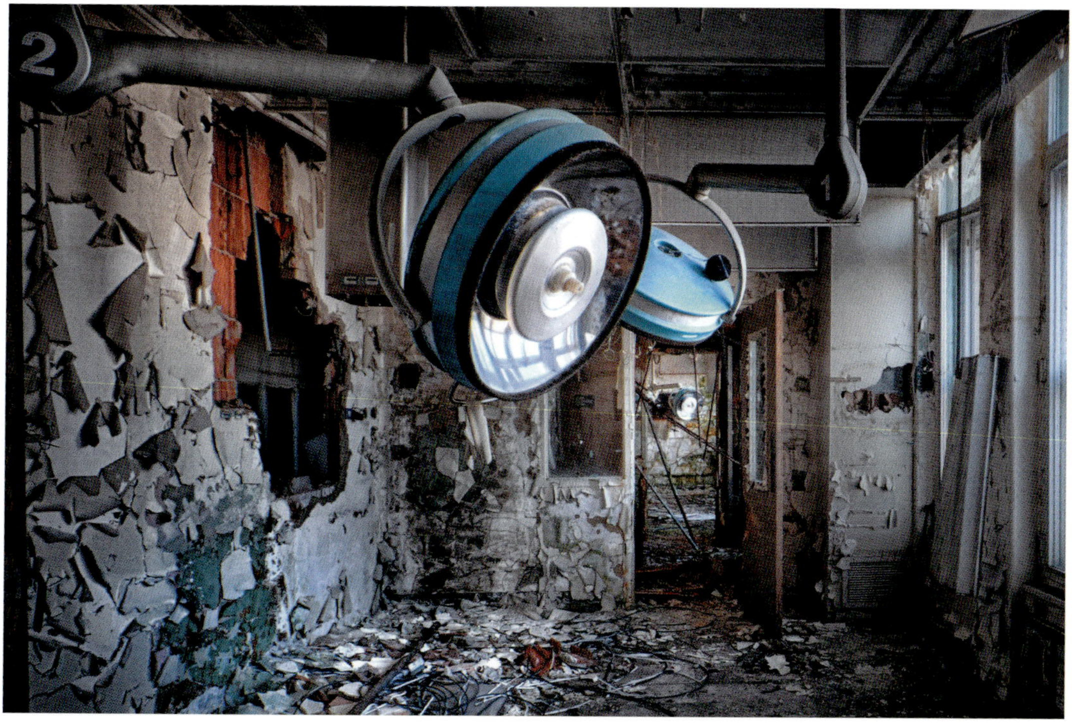

Please, inhale deeply and begin to count backwards from one hundred.

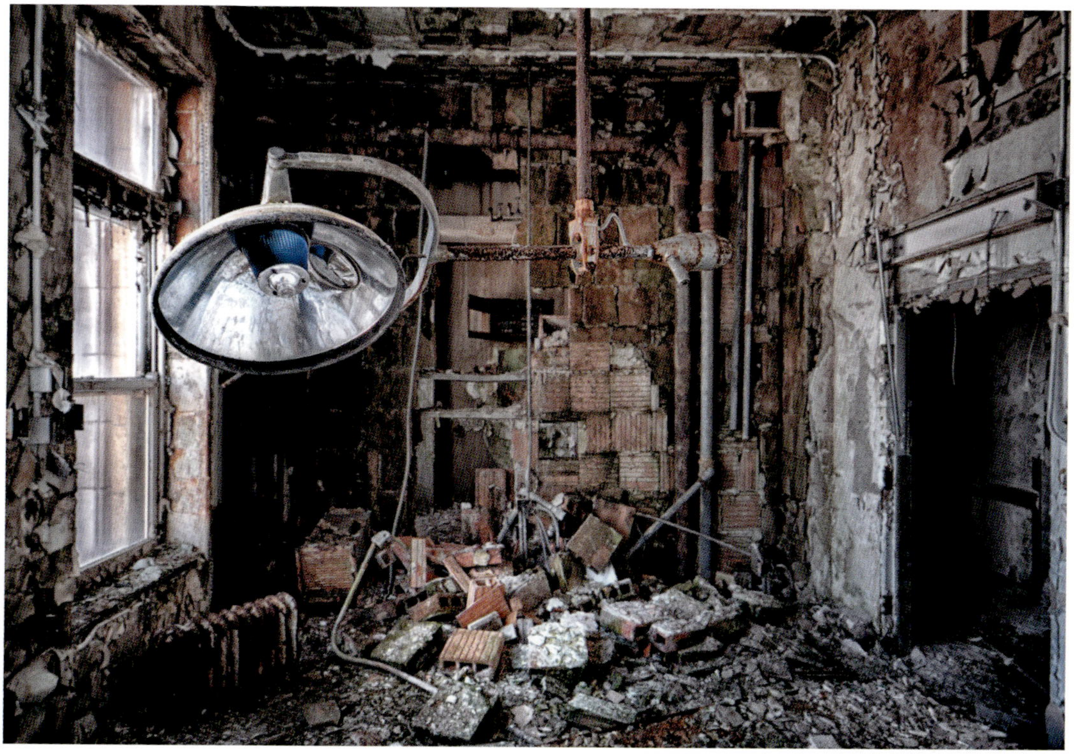

Tell me your pain on a scale of one to ten.

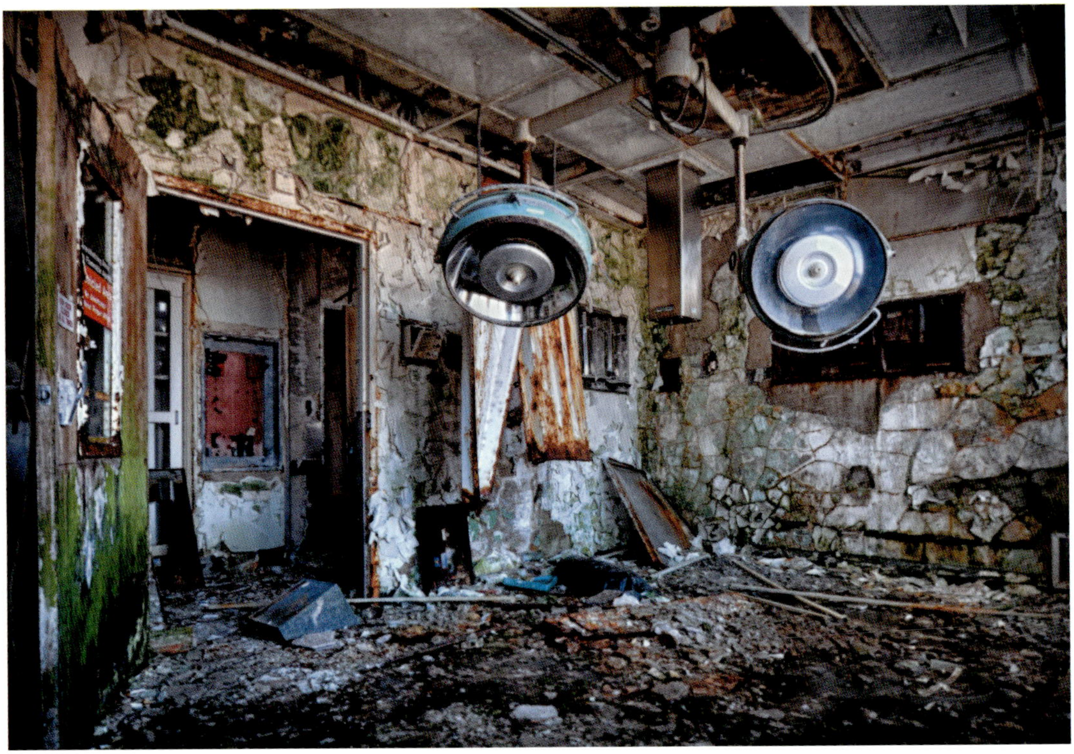

You're going to feel a little pressure now.

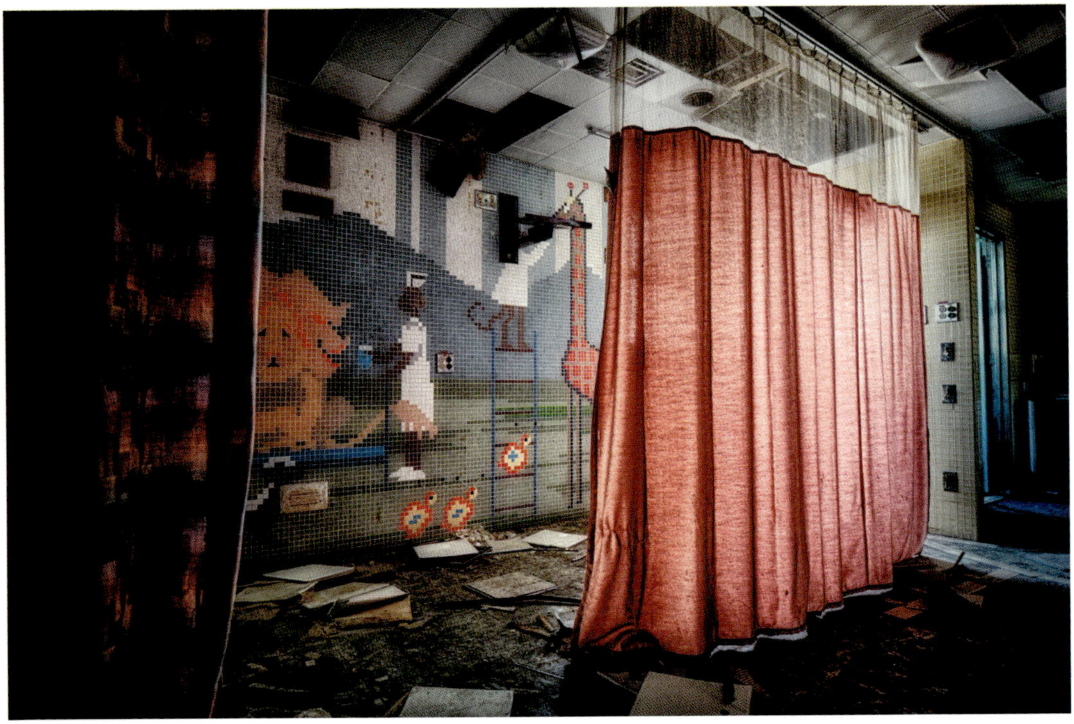

Jeez, even the lion is sad.

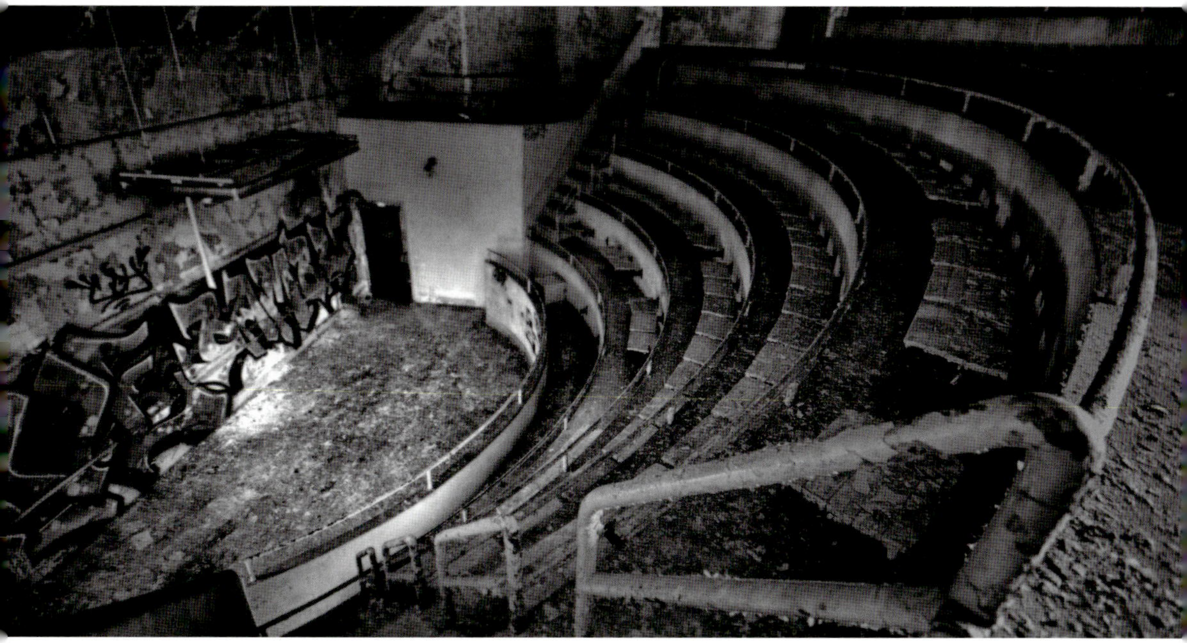

A surgical theater remained on the top level of this Chicago hospital.

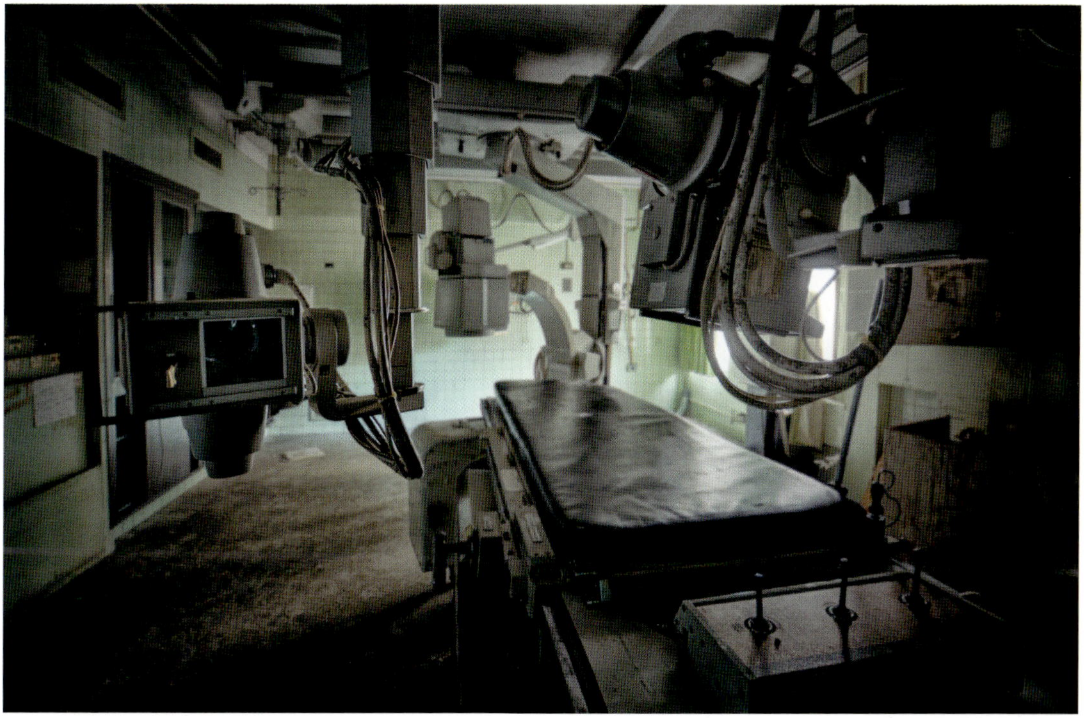

Radiology equipment can be unnerving in the right light.

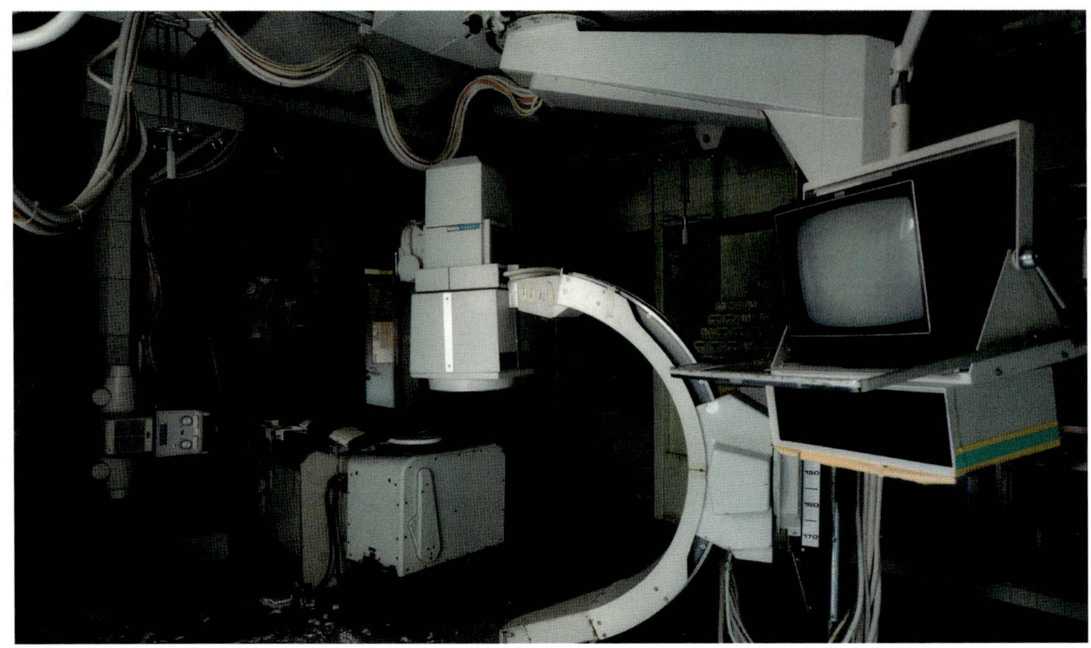

Radiology equipment can be unnerving in any light, frankly.

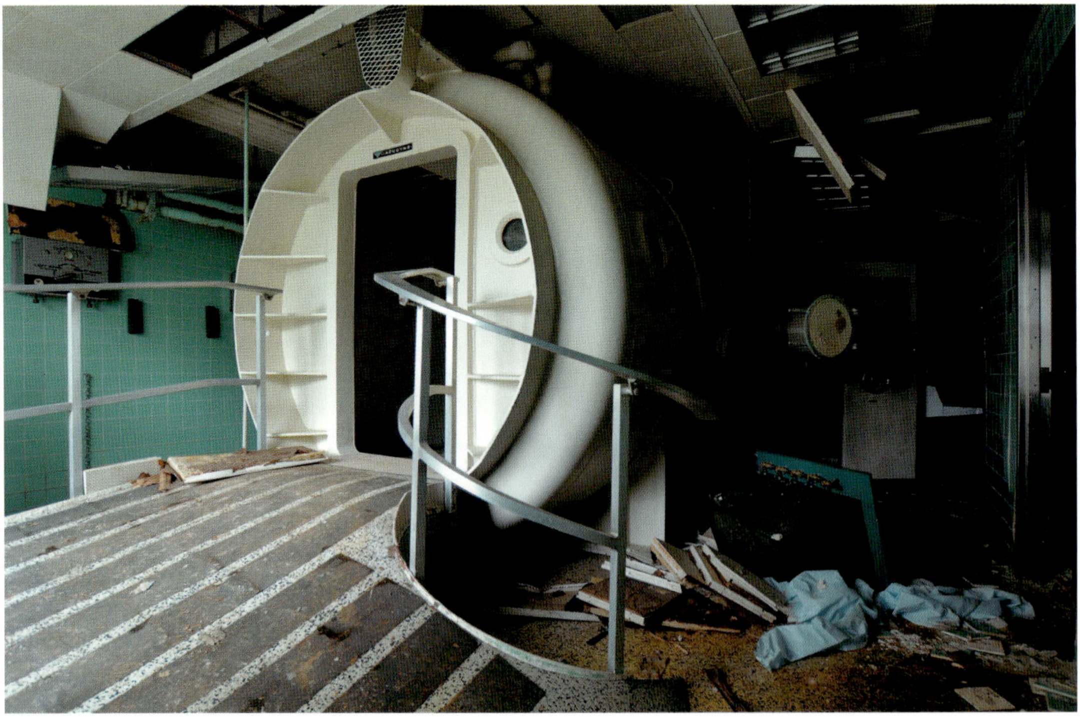

Those ugly deep-sea fish that kind of look like Jimmy Durante are stored here so they don't explode.

Power plants are hard to miss; they tend to be large industrial sites with tall smokestacks visible from far around. Most people have only seen them from the outside, and then usually at a distance. The fossil fuel burning ones are, thankfully, slowly losing ground to clean energy options, but are still commonplace. They are big out of necessity; to produce the power that modern cities need, mountains of coal must get burned in giant boilers, which will produce the steam necessary to spin the enormous turbine generators. Thus, even this relatively small plant in Chicago's southern suburbs is cavernous.

This was another place I spent lots of time in early on. Though even then it had been abandoned over four decades, it retained all the machinery within, though much worse for wear. For a beginning urbex photographer, it was a perfect place to visit and practice the craft; everywhere were objects of differing colors and textures, and light varied from adequate higher up to near-abject gloom on the lower floors. Even the local authorities, a perpetual concern, were unusually hands-off with trespassers. Once we were summoned from within by a police bullhorn, and were sure that arrest awaited us outside. After a brief and nervous conference, we decided there was no way to escape back to the car unnoticed, and we were just going to have to march outside and face the music. The officer that confronted us simply chided us for being careless; before letting us go, he told us that the next time we came to visit, we should at least call ahead to the police and let them know we would be spending time inside the plant.

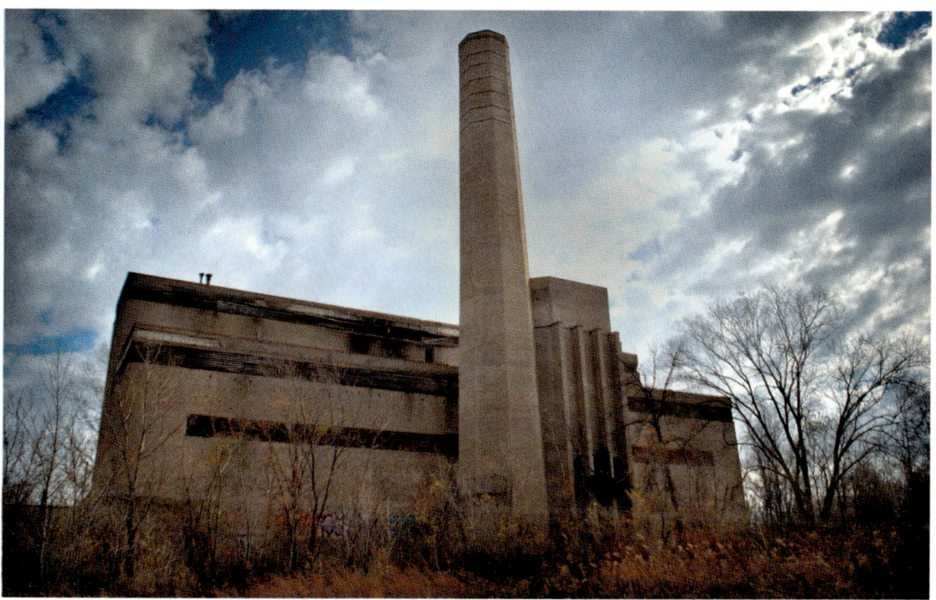

Mighty powerhouse of industry, seen from the west.

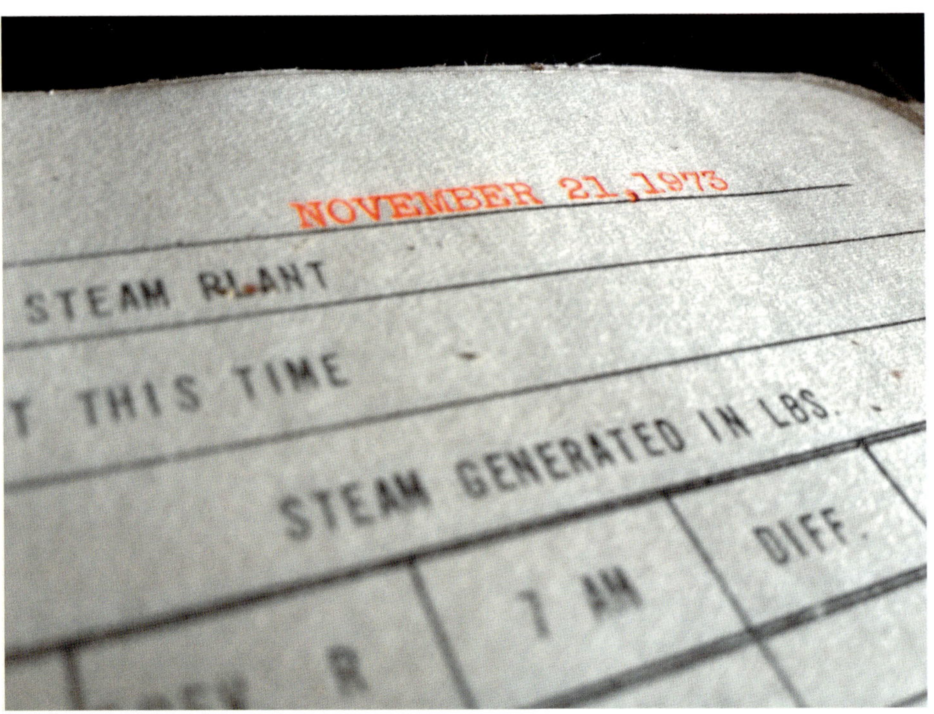

These were the latest records I could find.

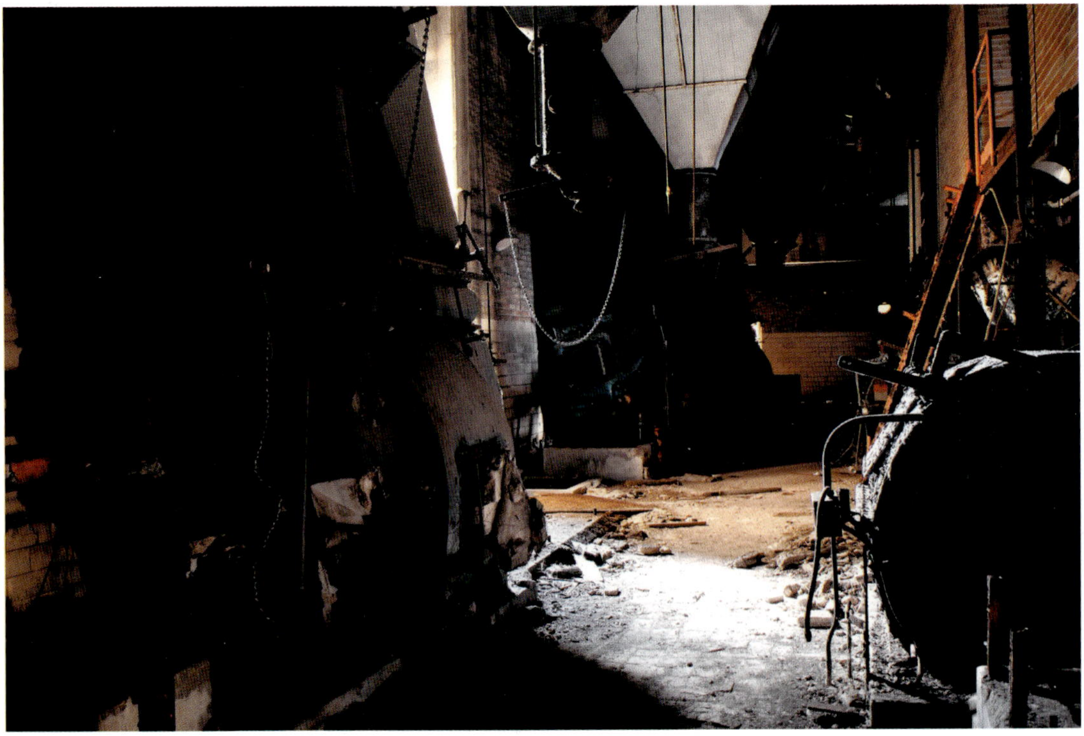

Main plant floor.

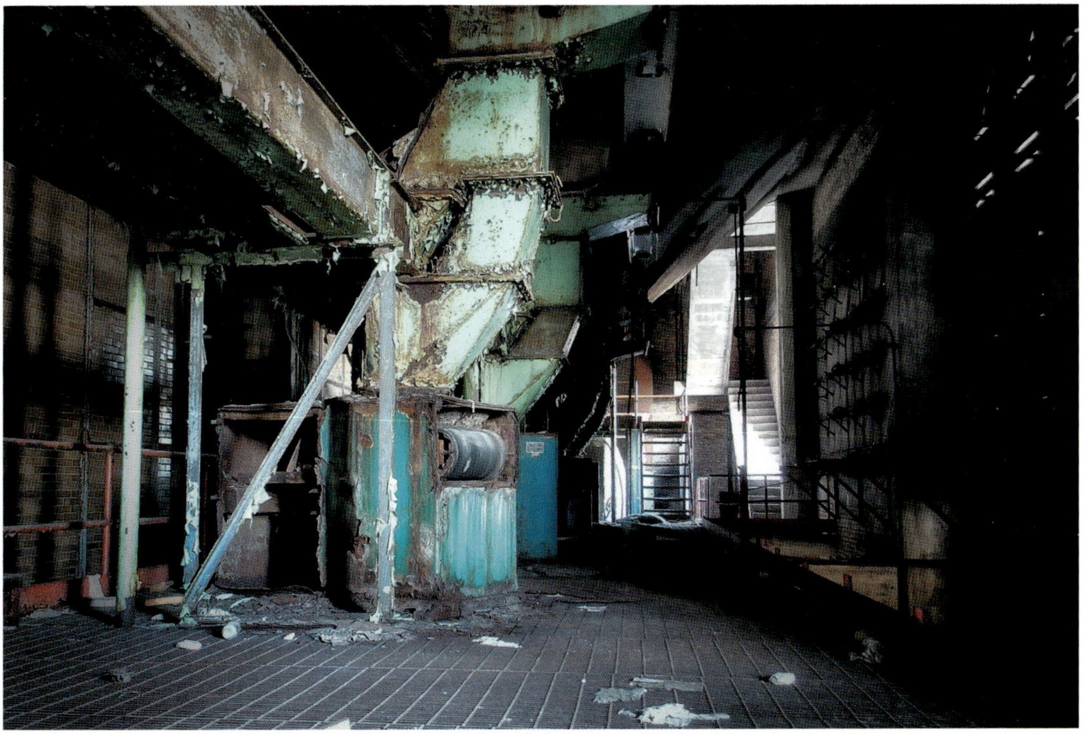

Second-floor catwalk.

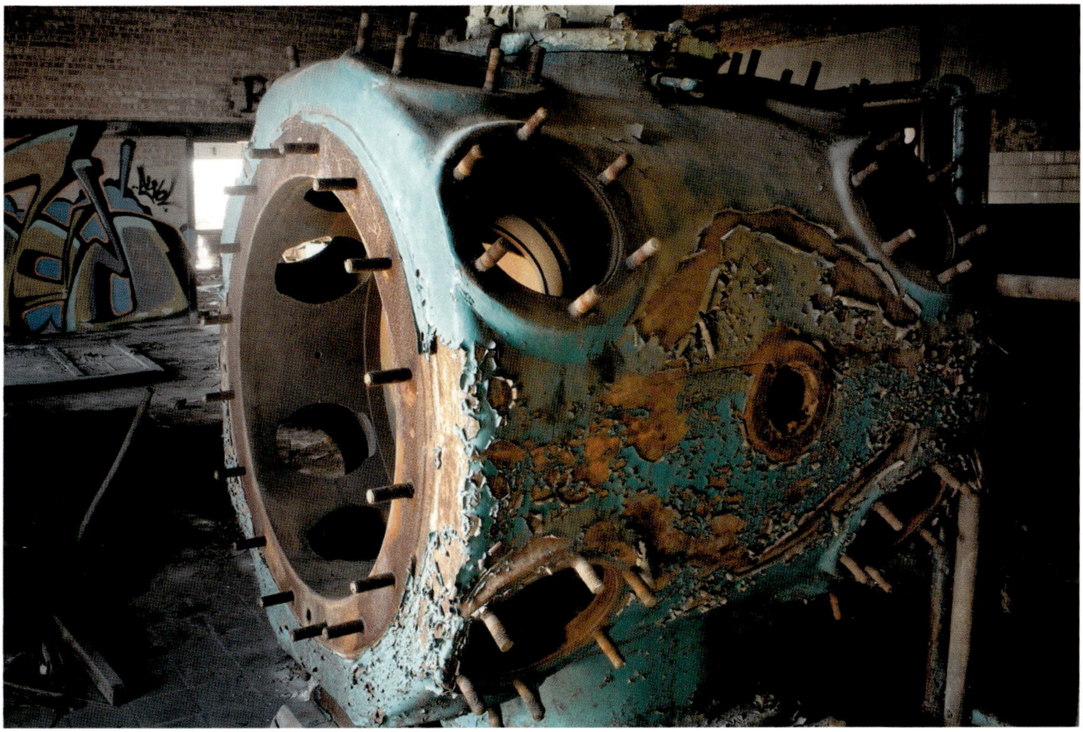

Machinery.

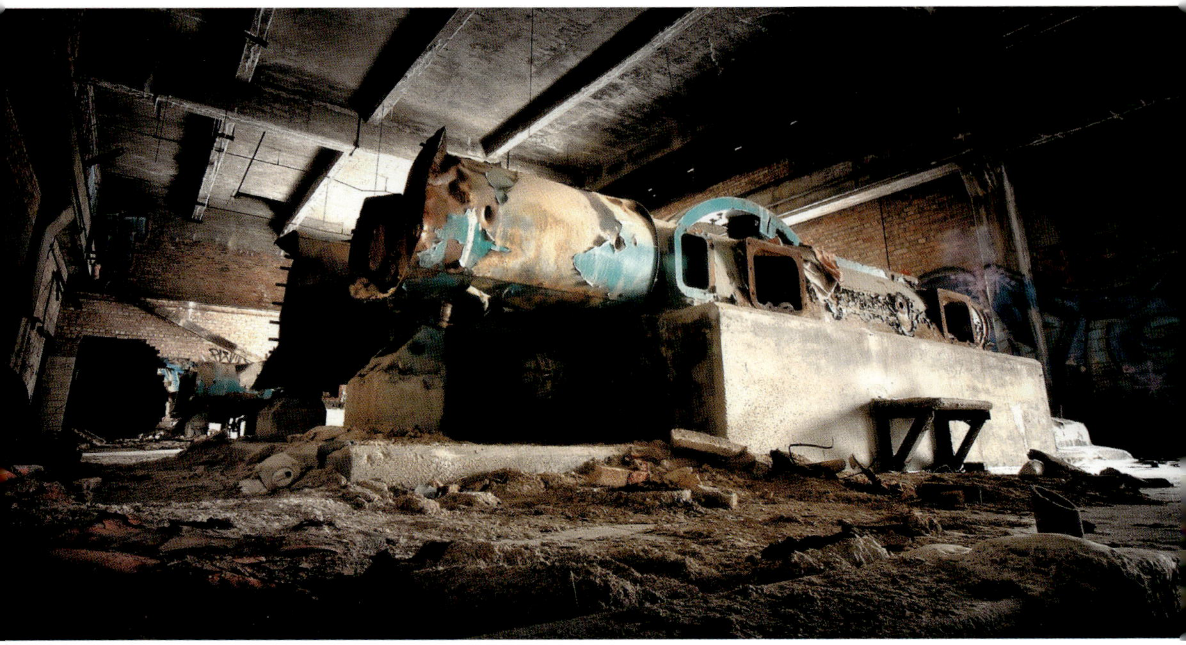

Turbine room.

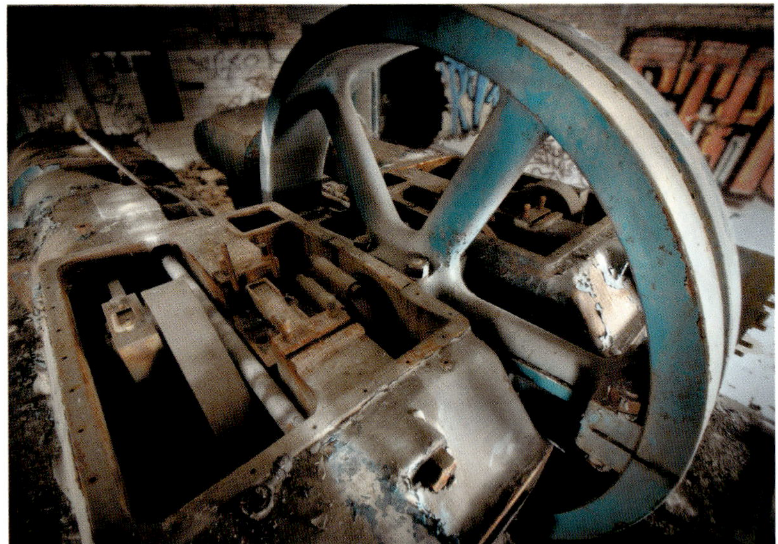

Flywheel.

In another life, I might have been an actor. As it is, I get to channel my dramatic tendencies into photography, and only get to spend time backstage when the theater is abandoned. Not a bad deal, though, as abandoned theaters, especially the stage areas, can be as dramatic as the works that were performed on them.

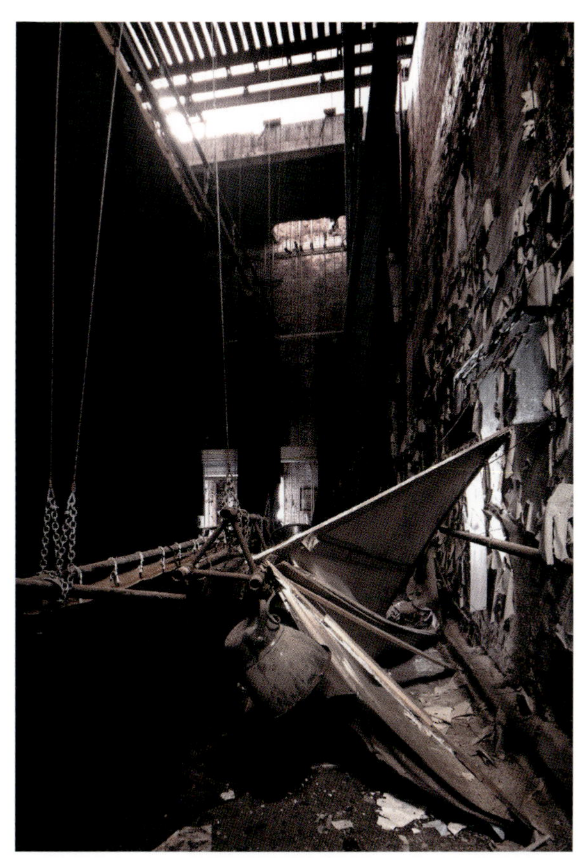

Left: Backstage.

Below: Stage rigging.

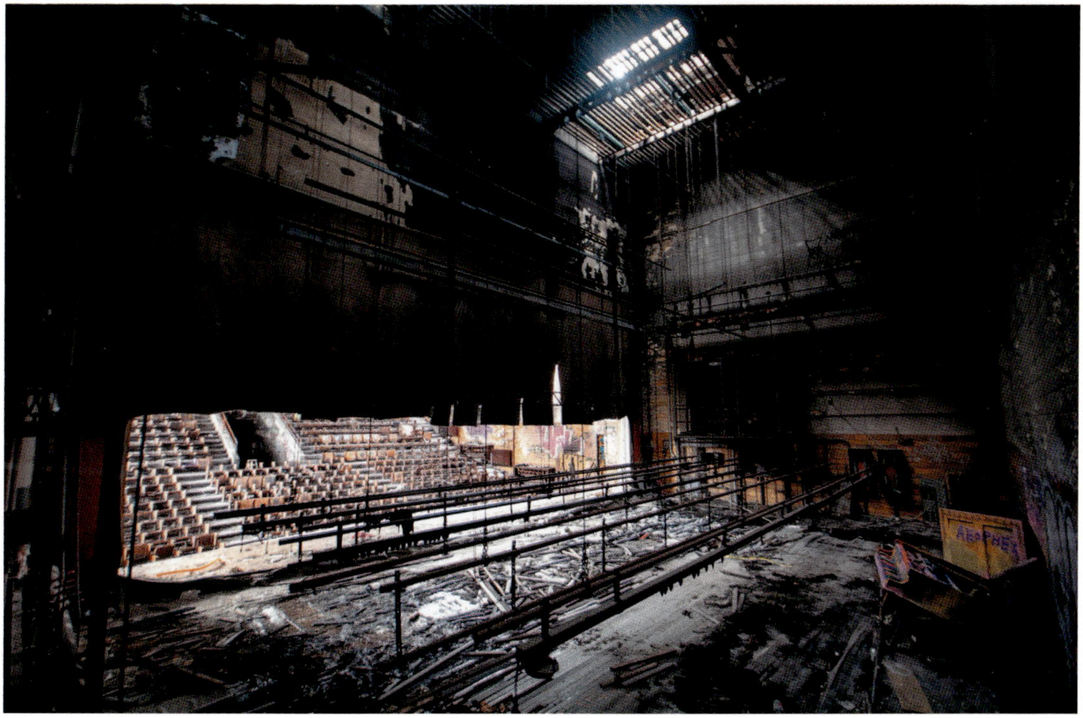

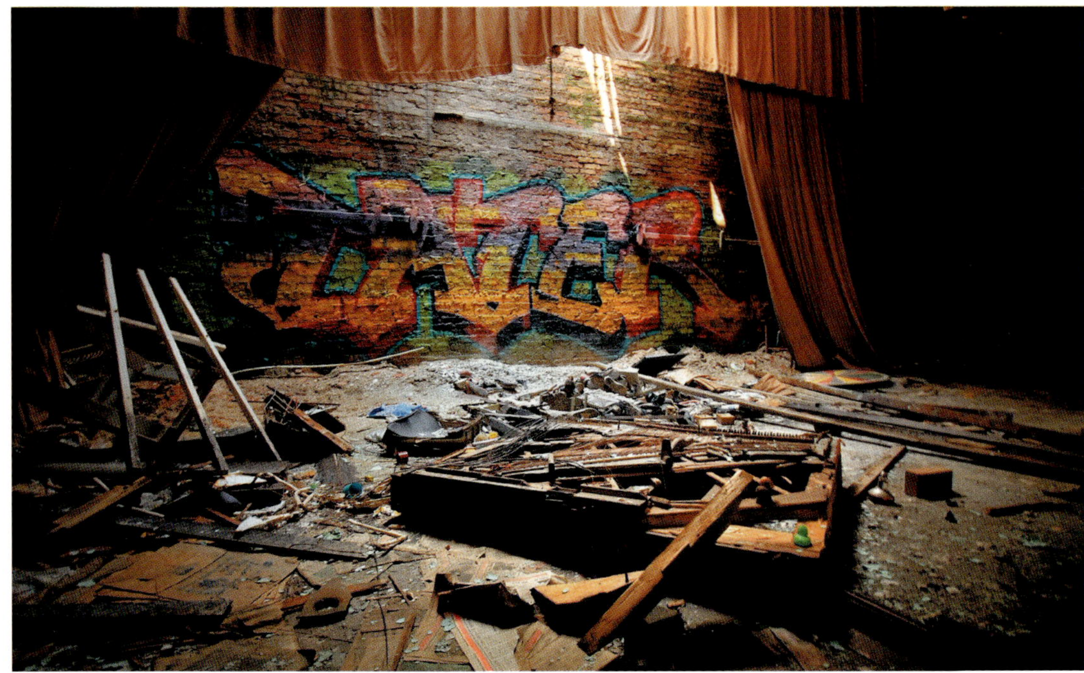

Dying piano being summoned by Heaven.

Post offices may be on the list of places the average person can't just walk into off the street, but it's unclear how many people would actually want to. The postal service has a rather staid reputation that brings to mind waiting in line or disinterested employees rather than anything exciting. But when the employees leave and the building gets left to time and the elements, that may be another story. This was, after all, a government office. How many workplaces have a walk-in safe emblazoned with the seal of the United States?

The particular architecture of this post office in northwest Indiana laid the ground for what would become a spectacular sight much later. Between the loading docks on one end and the customer service counter on the other, the ground level consisted mainly of a large open floorplan. The wood floor was made of short blocks cut across the grain and inlaid mosaic style, rather than the usual long strips of board running alongside each other. This was a rather common way of flooring factories and workspaces at the time of the building's construction, and was said to be a more forgiving surface, as well as more easily modified and relaid whenever heavy machinery needed to be moved or replaced. Above this floor was a sawtooth roof, which allowed the maximum amount of natural light to filter in. This light, later coupled with rain as the roof decayed, would turn pockets of the floor into greenhouses, as verdant mosses and shrubs grew out of the rotting floor. The effect of these islands of emerald blossoming in the gloom is quite striking.

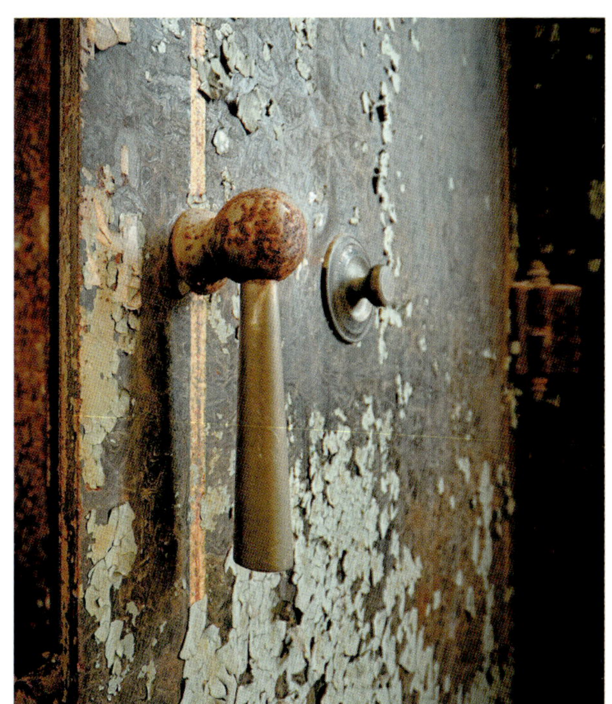
Safe door.

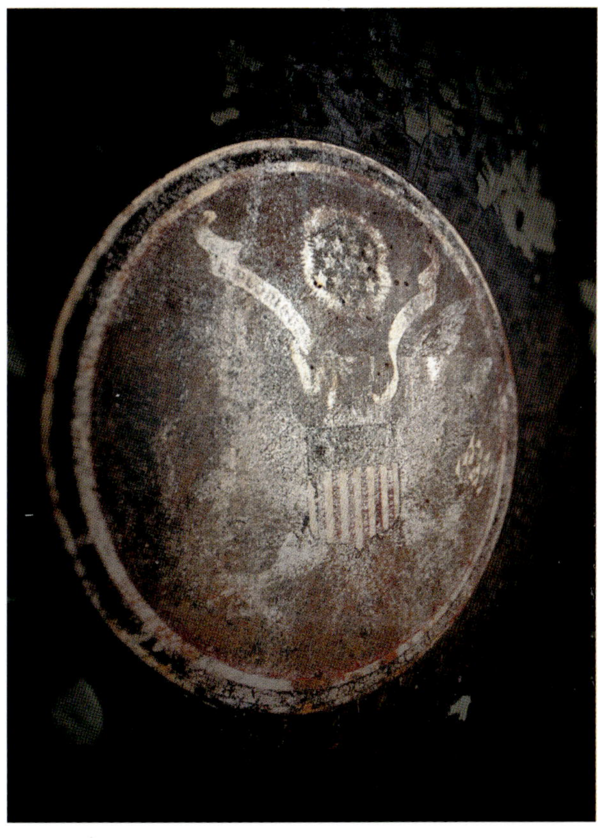
Seal detail.

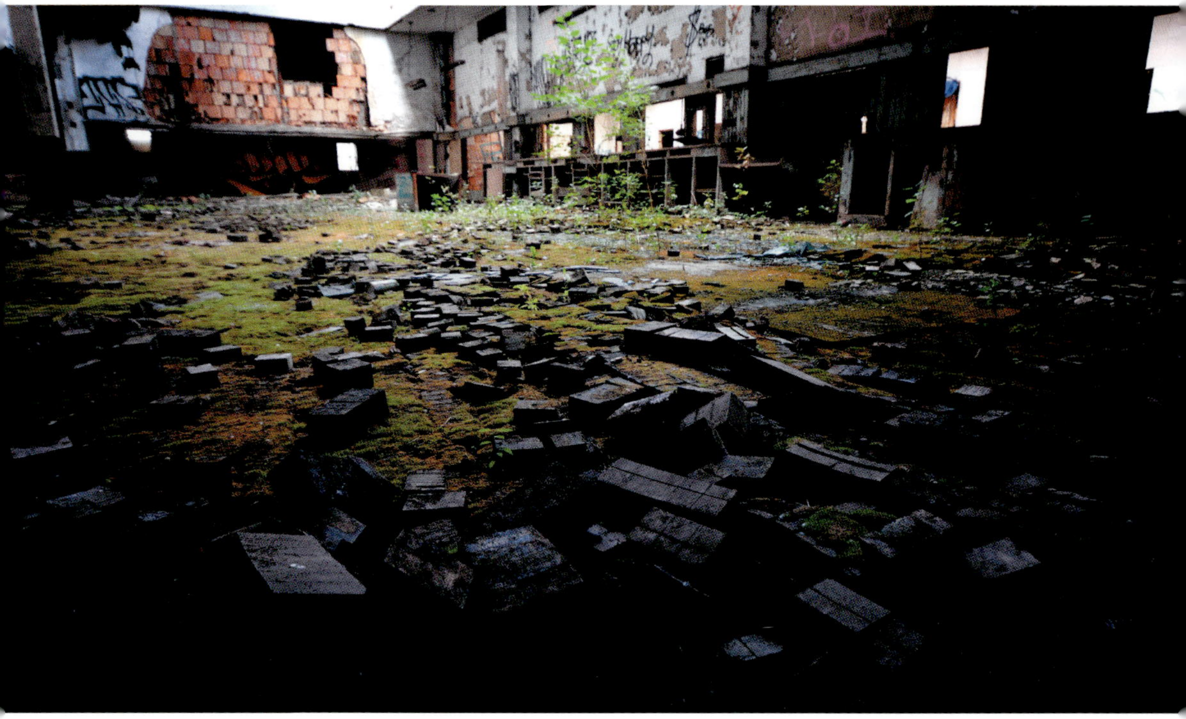

Post office floorscape.

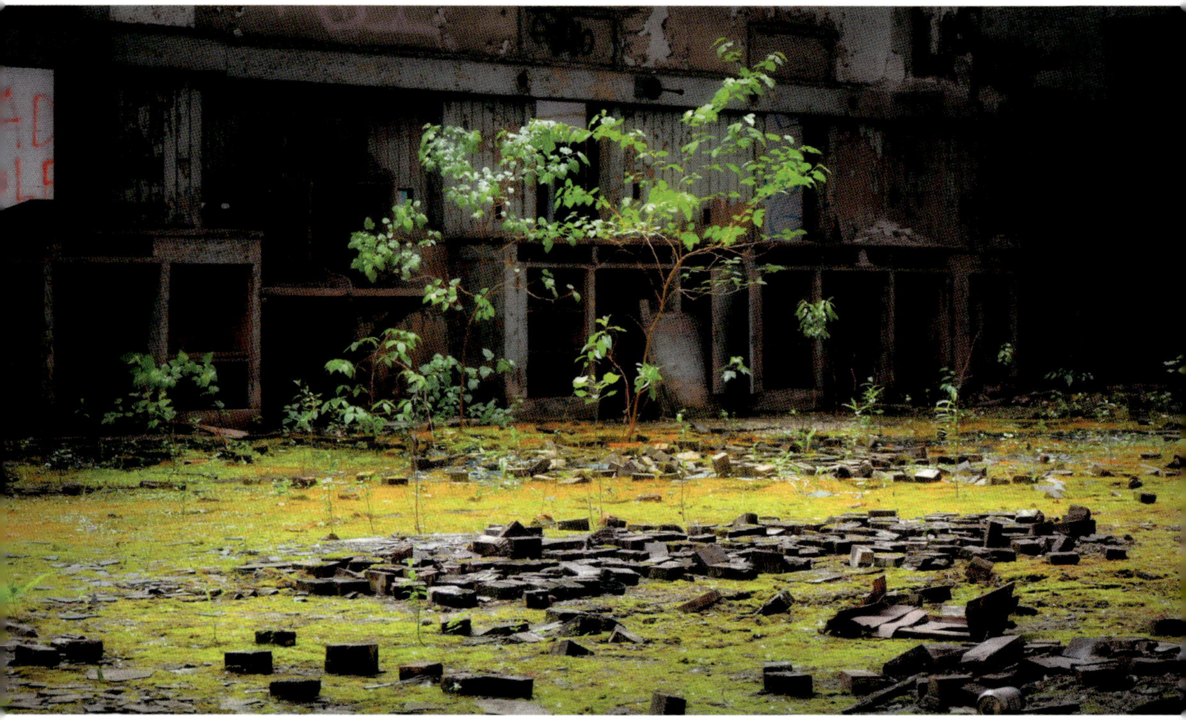

A pool of green and light.

Some naysayers may point out that there is nothing "off-limits" about a bank vault, or that anyone, for a modest fee, may rent a safety deposit box for themselves. These people should be ostracized and their words unheeded, as these rich fat cats will be first against the wall when the revolution comes, and the contents of their vaults reappropriated to the masses anyhow. Won't they look foolish, having quibbled with the finer details of a book on photography, instead of atoning for their class sins! Their bitcoins and rubies will one day adorn temples of learning erected for the benefit of the proletariat!

Ahem.

I had never myself been inside a bank vault, and so was suitably impressed by the space. Though this bank in Gary had been abandoned a while, the various little doors and cubbies were all in working order. Even the massive vault door looked like it could be swung closed and locked with a little oiling to overcome the rust's resistance. It was another area that was hard to shoot, with sunlight from the bank's distant front door creating glare and shadows that had to be worked around. The end results involved a little light painting and a bit of postprocessing afterwards, but hopefully showcase this place well.

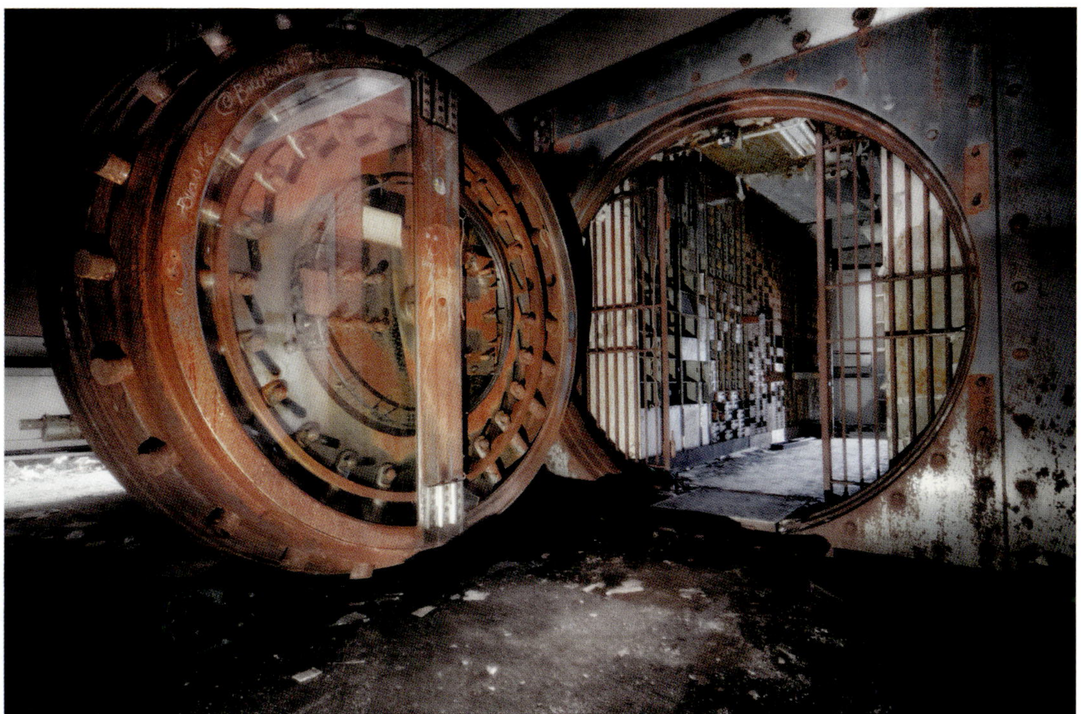

Vault.

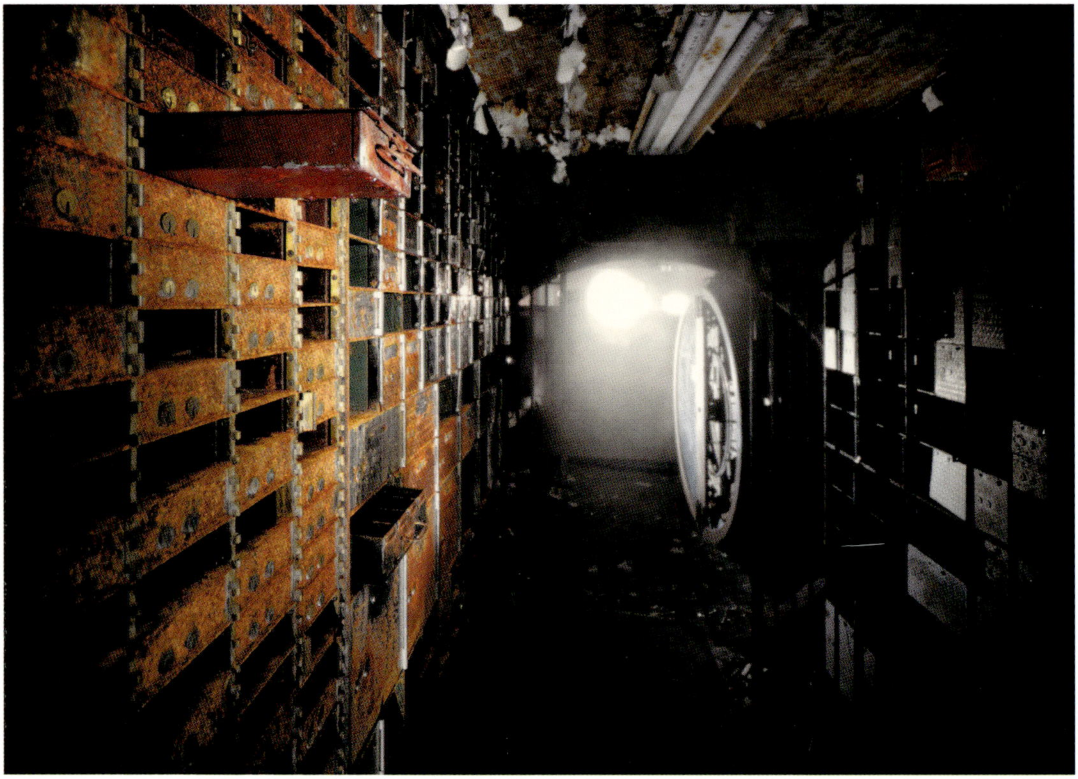

If you can't beat the glare, embrace it.

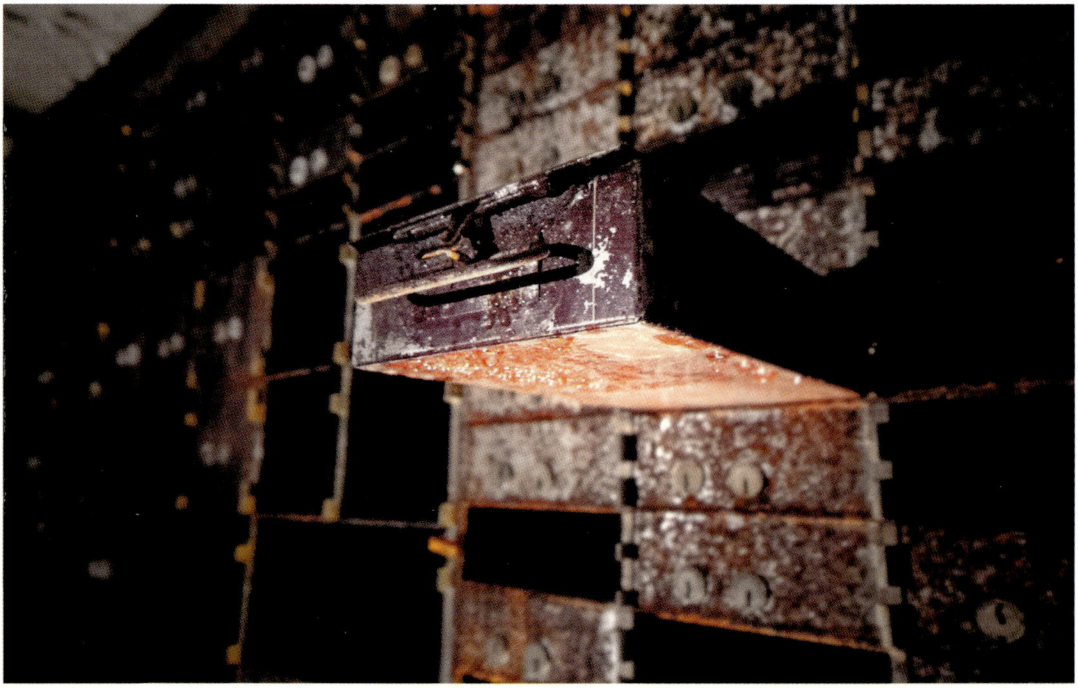

Deposit box detail.

It is true that just how "off-limits" a place is a little subjective. The church tower in the shot below was from a Chicago church that, at the time, was still technically open, though mass was no longer being held there while the diocese tried to decide on the feasibility of renovation. That said, the friendly deacon stationed inside the front doors who invited visitors to look around probably would not have approved of one such visitor climbing into the clock tower.

On the other hand, this former southside candy factory seemed like an easy exploration, until we tried leaving. It was then that were confronted by a couple security vehicles that had been lying in wait for us. We managed to duck back inside and, eventually, give them the slip, but the lesson was that you'll never know just how badly someone does not want you inside a building until you find out firsthand. Off-limits, indeed.

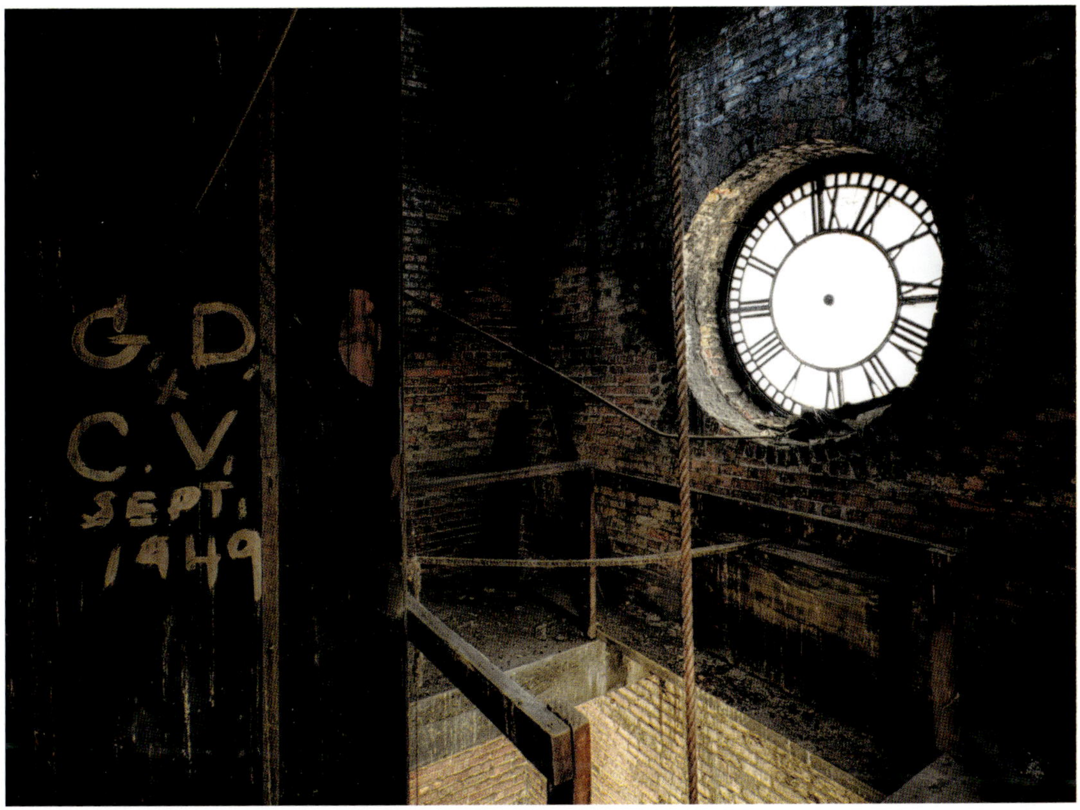

Fun trivia: the people whose initials are on the beam are now both dead.

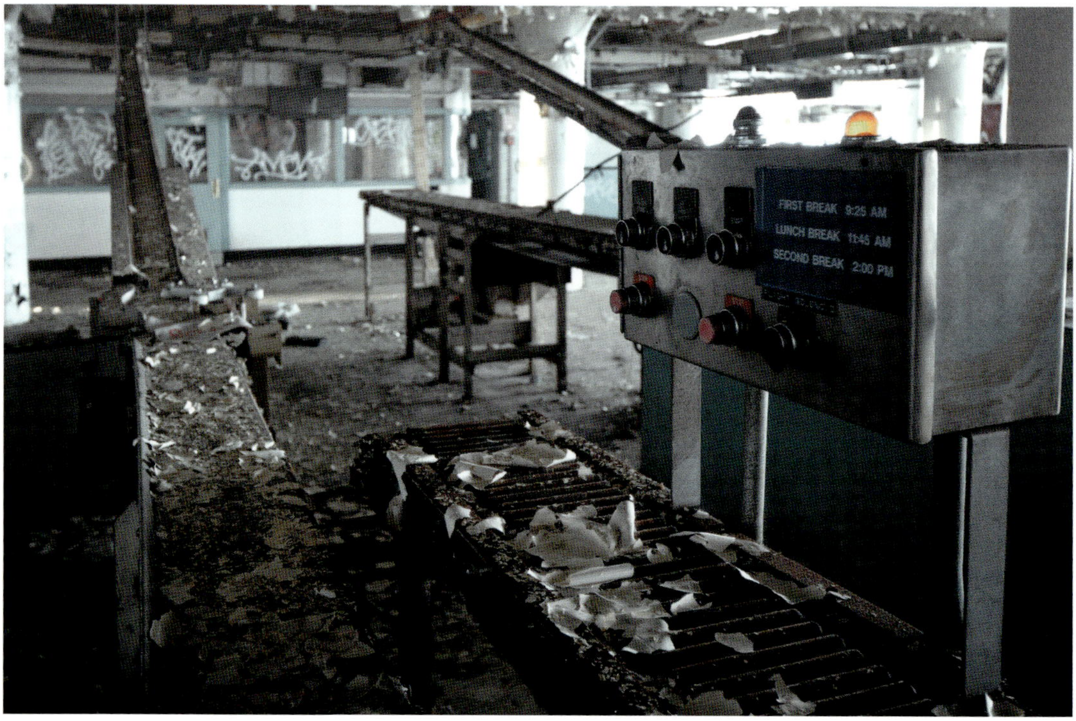

Union mandated breaks are important for one's mental wellbeing, lest the crushing banality of existence collapse on one like an imploding septic tank.

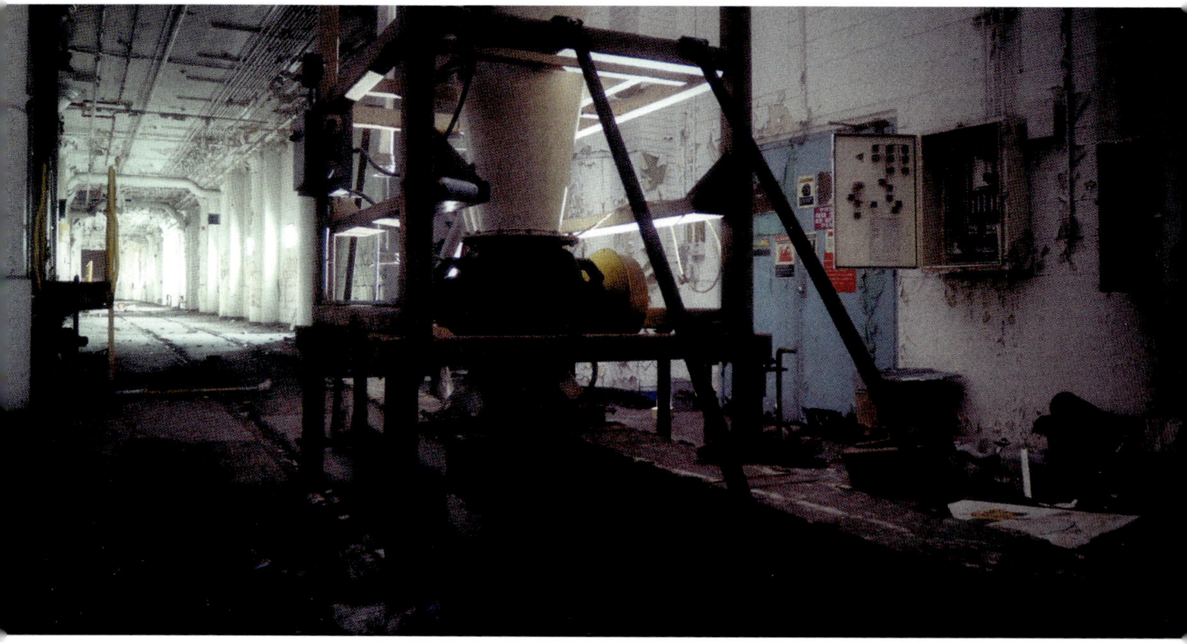

Children, there is candy down that hallway.

8

DETAILS AND THE DEVILS WITHIN THEM

What often tells the tale of a building's former existence are the things left behind. The architecture may be spectacular in its decrepit state, but it's these various objects that can be the strongest link to the past. Bricks and mortar can be impersonal, but somebody once handled these tokens of the past. As in the aforementioned case of hospitals, some things get left because they're impractical to move, but more often, the reasons are unknown. But, since objects can be arranged, staged, or brought from outside expressly for the purpose of enhancing a scene, the previously discussed issues of authenticity can crop up again. Luckily, outside props tend to be easy to spot, as the explorers that resort to such tactics are not usually subtle. I take for granted that many people may have come through before me and disturbed or ransacked a scene, so the issue of whether "native" objects have been rearranged is, for myself, an issue only if the effect is obvious. Rather, there are different concerns when shooting these objects.

Photographers are, naturally, drawn to this flotsam for the emotional resonance it has, with a plaintive framing of a lone object becoming a trope of its own within urbex photography. Tropes are useful as markers of conventions within a genre and may provide any artist a framework to work within or even creatively subvert. But too much of a trope becomes a cliché, and that is what brings us to the Lonely Chair.

It's not unusual to find chairs in the middle of wide open and otherwise empty rooms, framed by doorways, or otherwise posed for maximum dramatic effect. I've shot my share of these. But there are many urbex photographers out shooting today, and these pictures begin to look a bit similar. This isn't meant to be a harsh criticism of anyone in particular or the community at large, just to point out that with a little care, we can try to differentiate our work from those of others. Among examples of urbex tropes, the Lonely Chair may be foremost, but there's many others. A personal favorite is pianos.

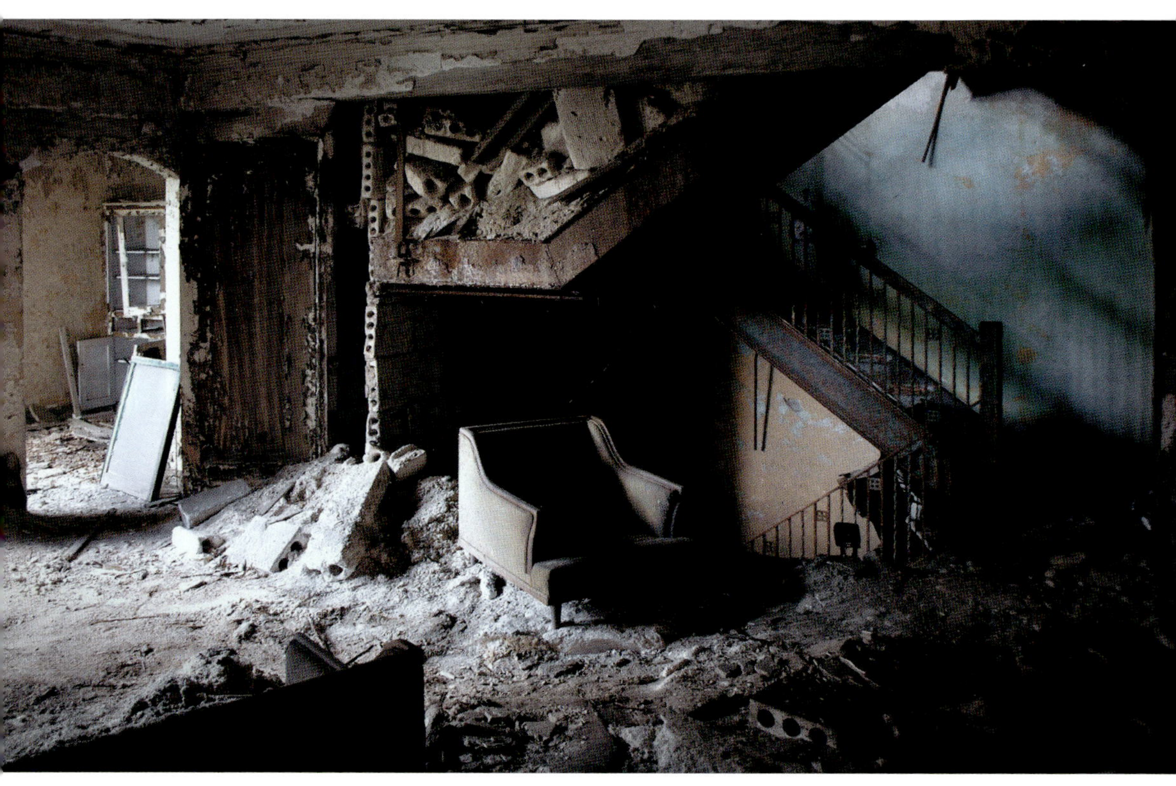

The Chair, as seen in its hermitage.

A joke between myself and a fellow explorer has been that, wherever we might go, there is always a piano present. Though not literally true, they tend to appear quite a bit. Almost every school hides one (or several, for that matter). Theaters and auditoriums have them as well, and churches or other houses of worship usually have an organ. I've come across them in more unusual places, too, but unfortunately for this book, not in Chicago.

Television sets are also common. Big, clunky consoles from the early eighties, with two large dials on the side, the second one for UHF, the whole thing encased in cheap wood veneer because it was supposed to be a piece of furniture. Televisions which, if one came across in the quiet gloom of abandonment, could still be heard making a slight static sizzle and with the faintest dying green point of light still floating in the middle of the screen. These are old, Reagan-era televisions.

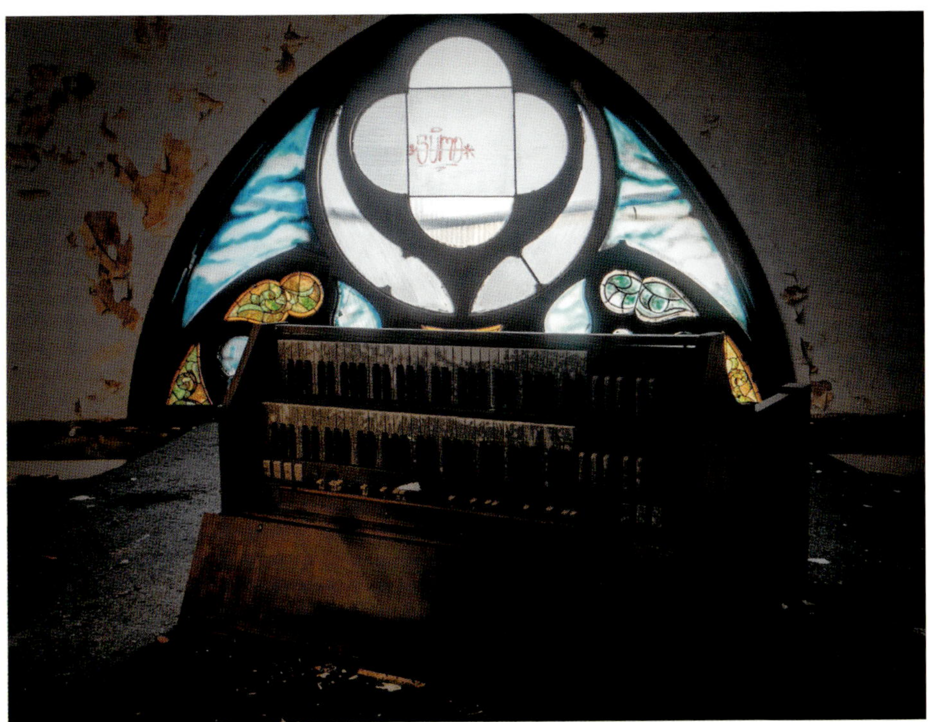

Church organ.

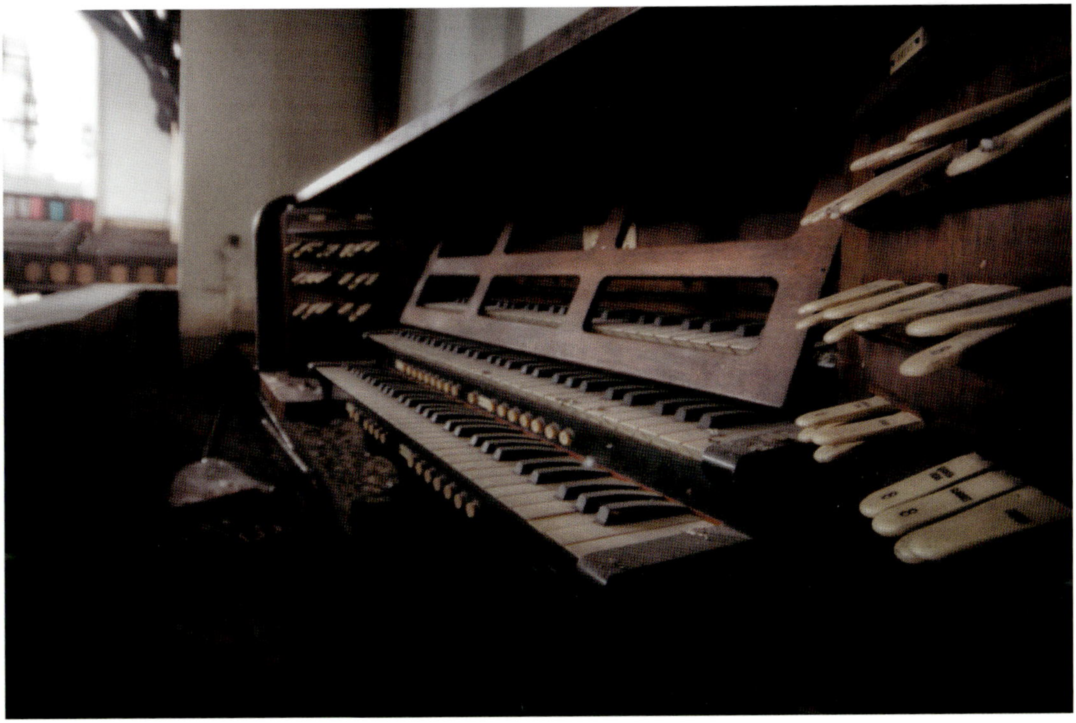

Fancier organ.

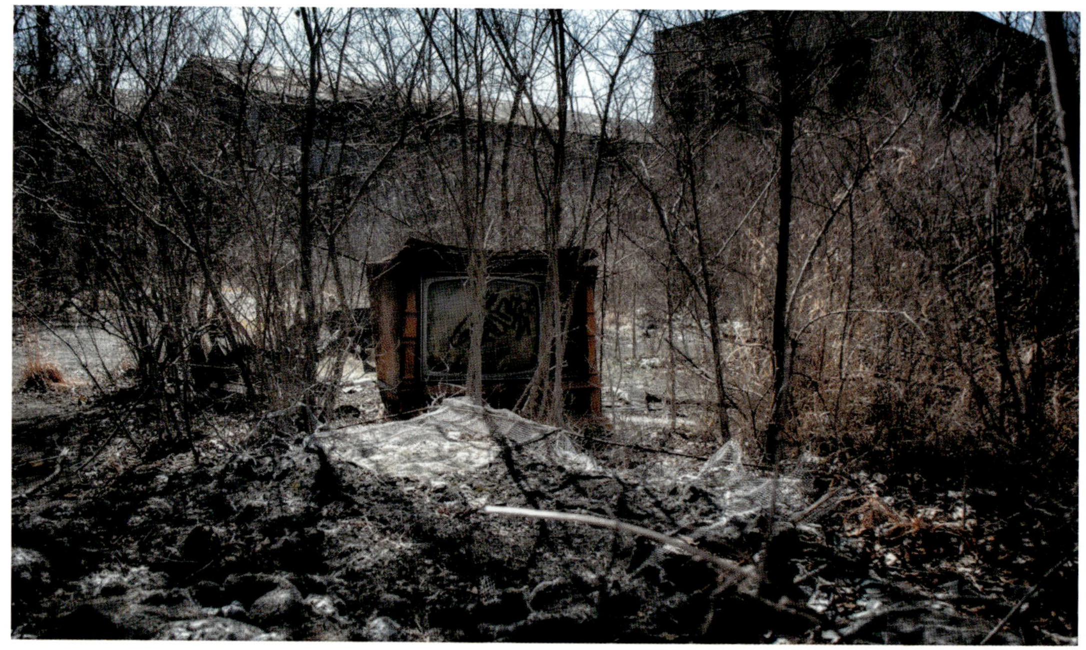

Outside of their natural environment of the family den, these magnificent sets are unable to camouflage or shelter themselves and are, sadly, quite prone to predation.

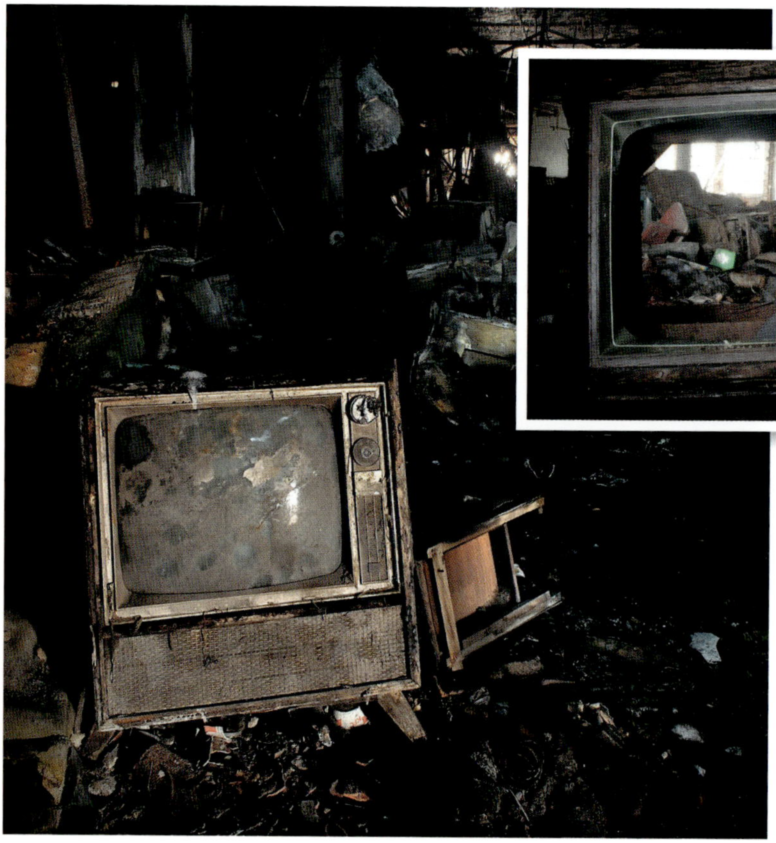

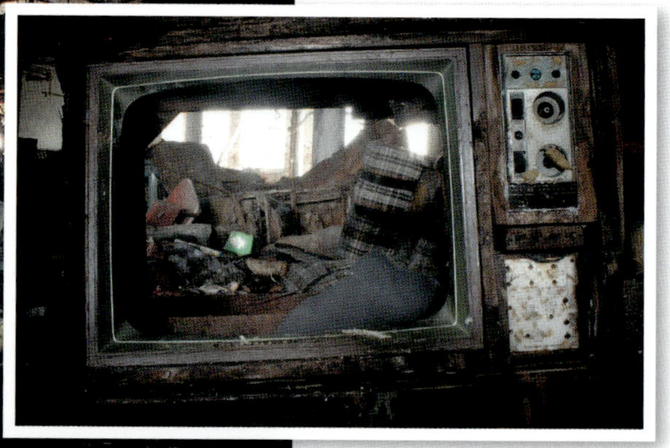

Many sets left at an old furniture store.

Fun fact: old television screens can explode if hit hard enough.

One of the sadder things I have seen while exploring is the sheer amount of materials left behind in schools, particularly in Gary. This isn't necessarily a result of negligence or malfeasance; as the city's population dwindled, many schools were shuttered in a short time span, and there's only so many things you can do with outdated textbooks or moldy novels. Still, the sight of roomfuls of books piled several feet high is affecting.

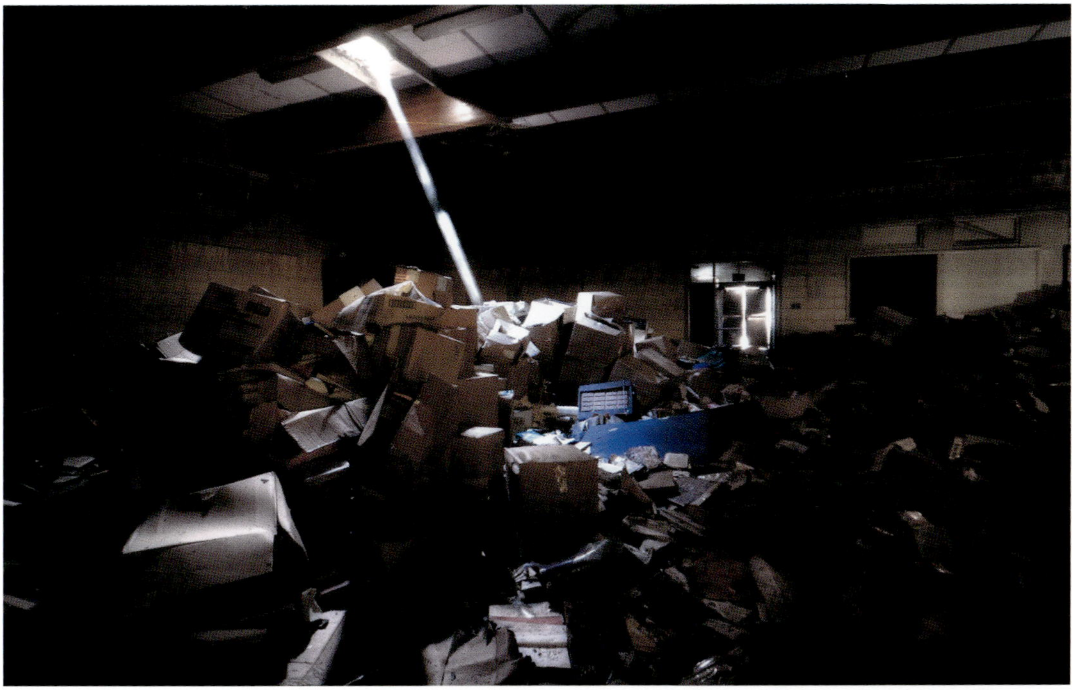

Mounds of books to the ceiling.

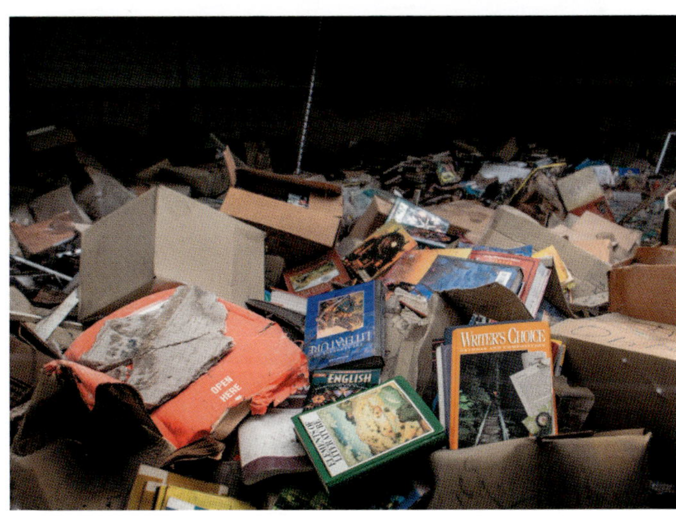

Boxes upon boxes across entire rooms.

From gyms strewn with dozens of broken computers, to the varied machines left behind in science labs, schools can be littered with the detritus of decades of students, teachers, and staff that once filled their hallways. Even the theater department's storage room in one Gary high school had thousands of costumes and props spilling out of every nook and cranny.

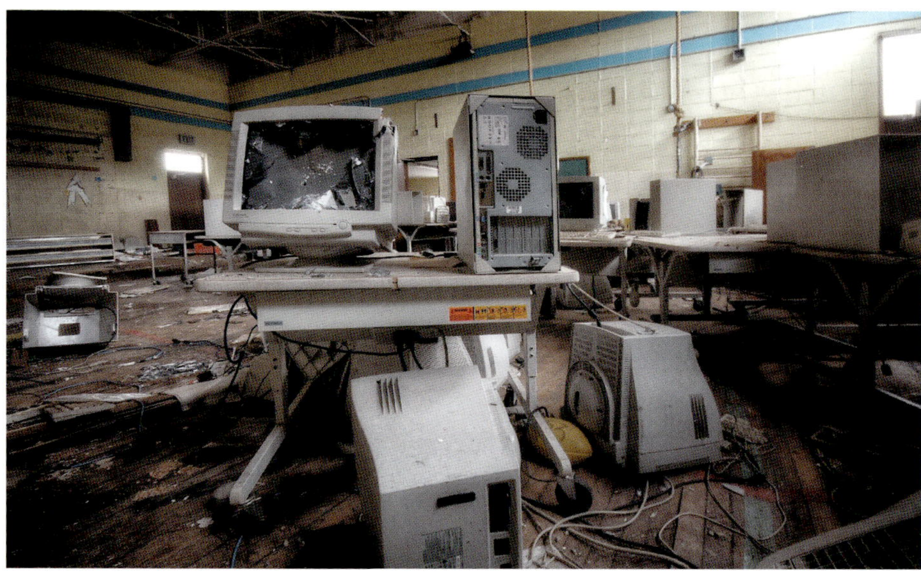

Computer graveyard.

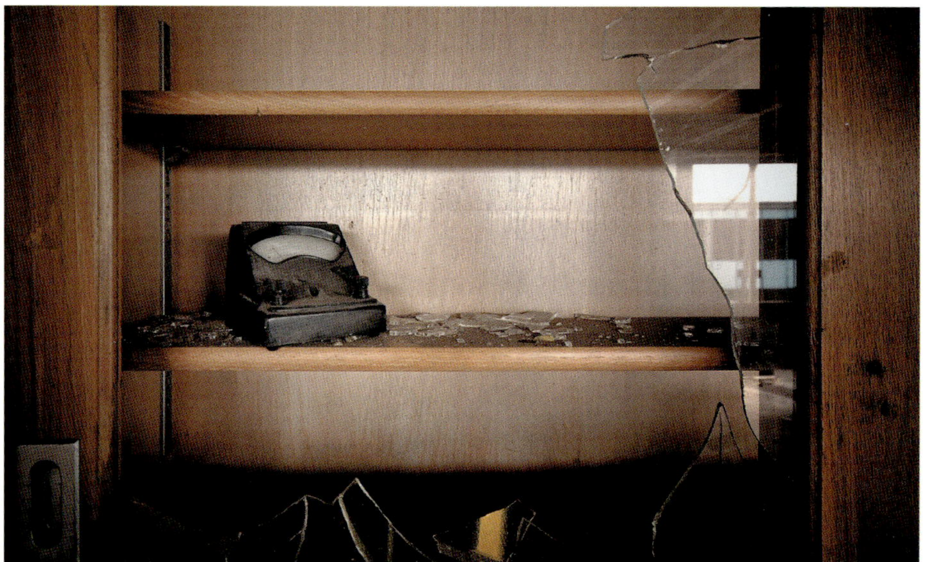

Science lab.

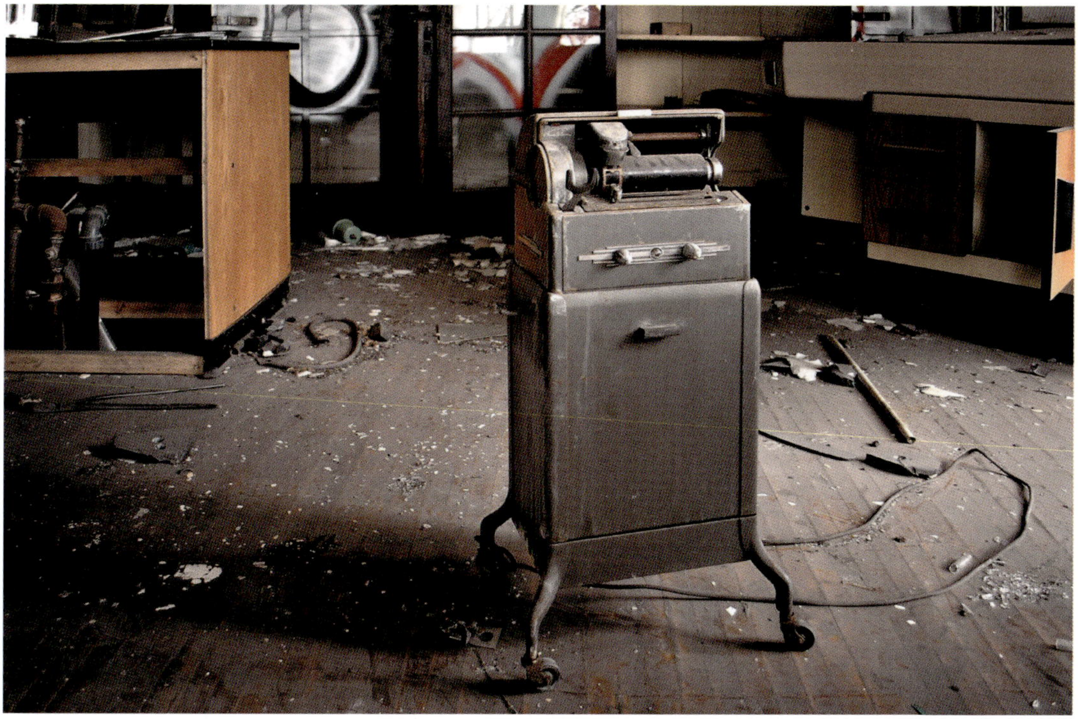

If I told you I knew what this was, I'd be lying to you.

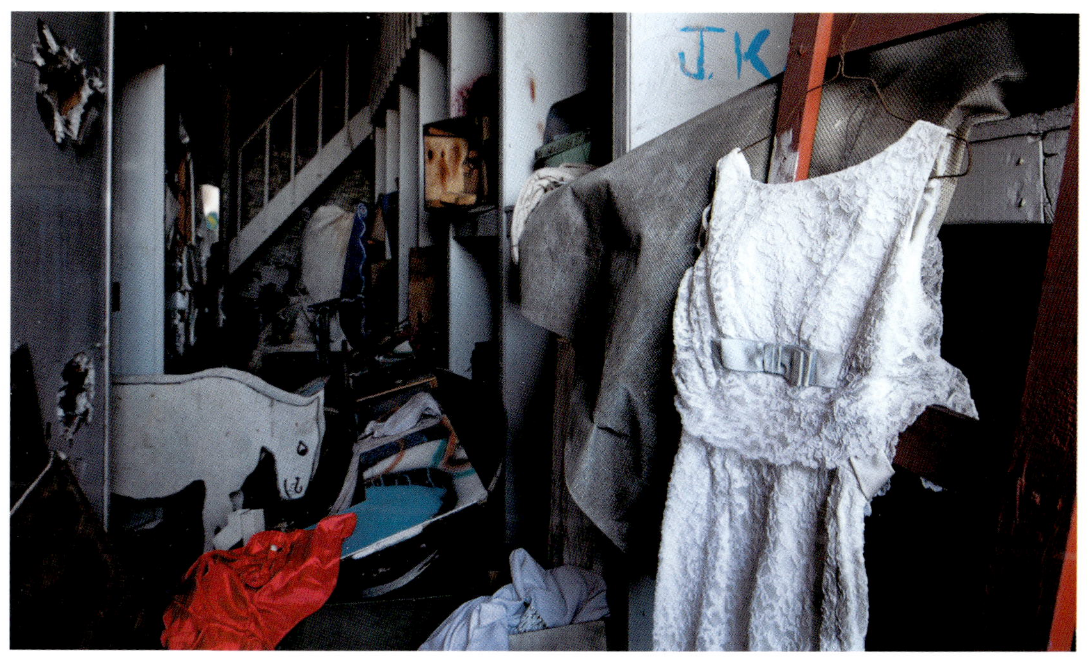

Drama, compartmentalized.

Less often do old factories around Chicago remain filled with the machinery that used to make them hum. In Rust Belt cities around the Midwest, a plant might get left for years as it was when it was shuttered, as there is little incentive for either the former owners or the surrounding community to do much with it. Here, if nothing else, the land the factory sits on may be valuable, so these places will be quickly stripped and razed to make room for something new. Consequently, more often what remain here are isolated hulks of steel that rise out of the floor in otherwise empty rooms.

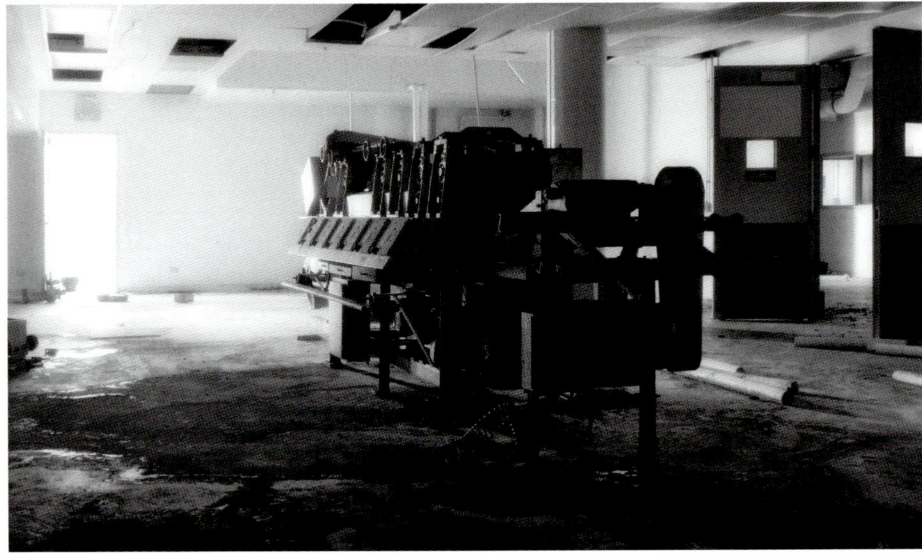

Machine purgatory.

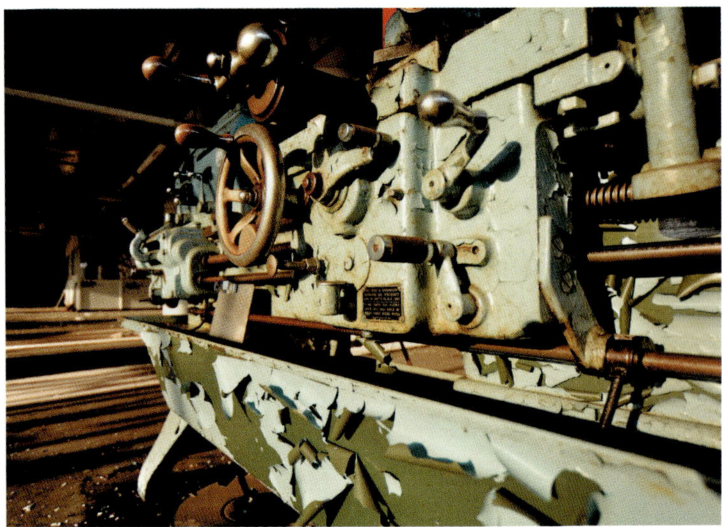

New trope: the Lonely Lathe.

Here are more of my favorite examples of things left behind around Chicago. There is the trinket left on the windowsill of an old home, a tricycle on the top floor of an old department store, and a rusting press left inside an old municipal print shop. This shop was within a larger, nondescript building that was still partially in use, next to an abandoned one I had been visiting for years; only a chance impulse led me try a door handle that turned out to be unlocked. The back room was completely dark, and only my flashlight showed the massive machine lurking in the dark. It is a strange feeling to come across a great find that you can't help but think you should have found years before, but it's better than not finding it at all.

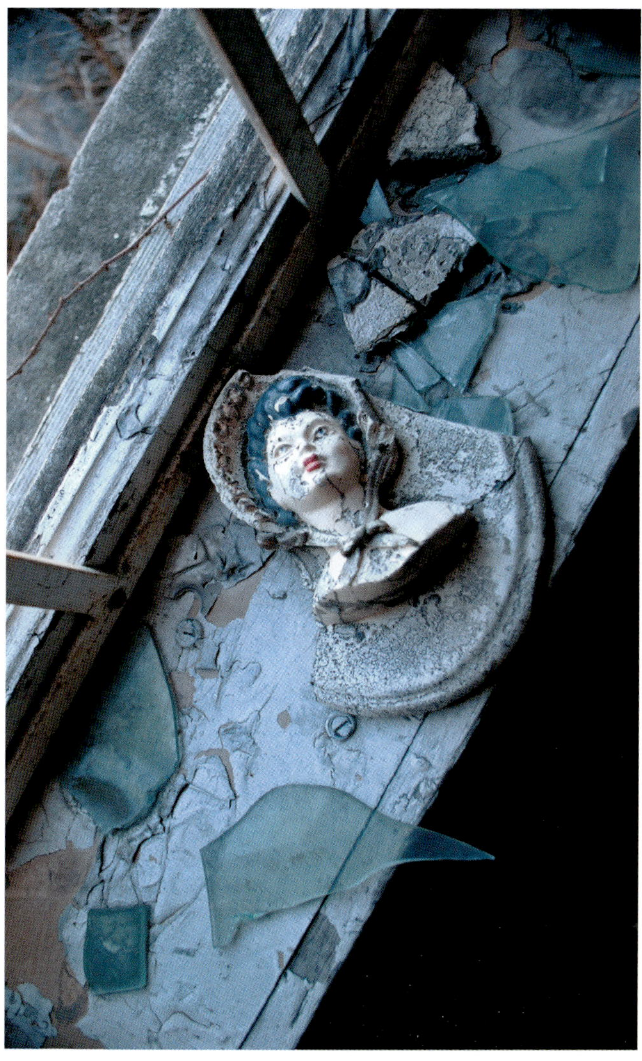

Wintertime windowsill gothic.

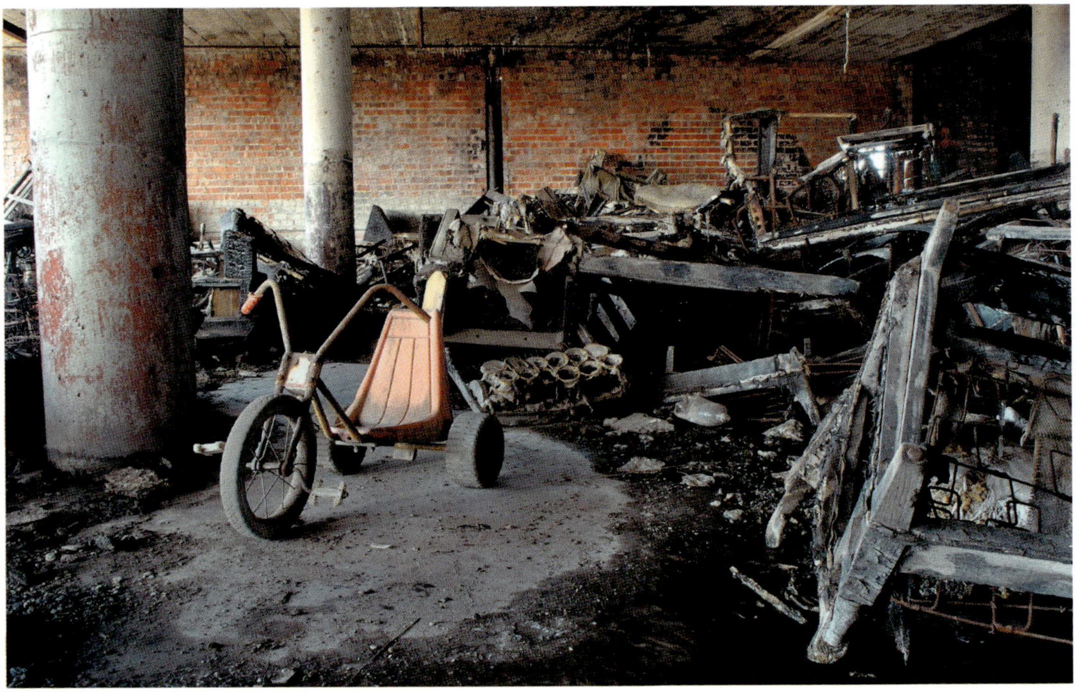

The tricycle of doom.

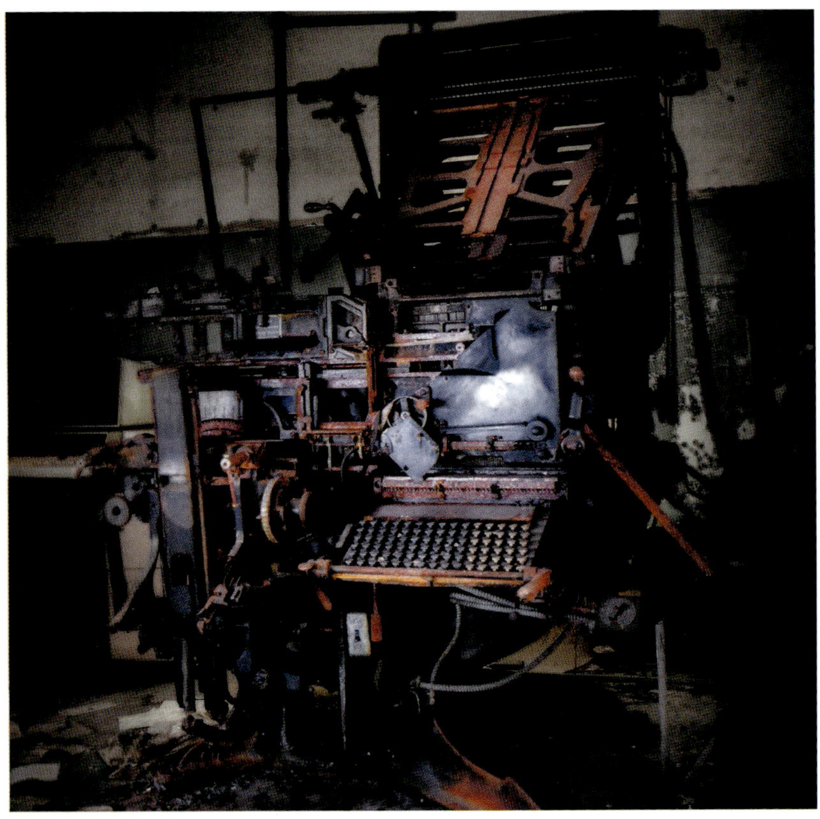

The printing press of foreboding.

Lastly, there is a Marine Corps jet that sits out in a far-flung suburb. An acquaintance, knowing the nature of my hobby, tipped me off on where it could be found. I will confess that this plane doesn't truly qualify as abandoned, as it sits in someone's backyard. That said, I think it's safe to assume it won't be leaving this spot, much less flying, anytime soon. And how often does one get to see an old military airplane sitting out like this?

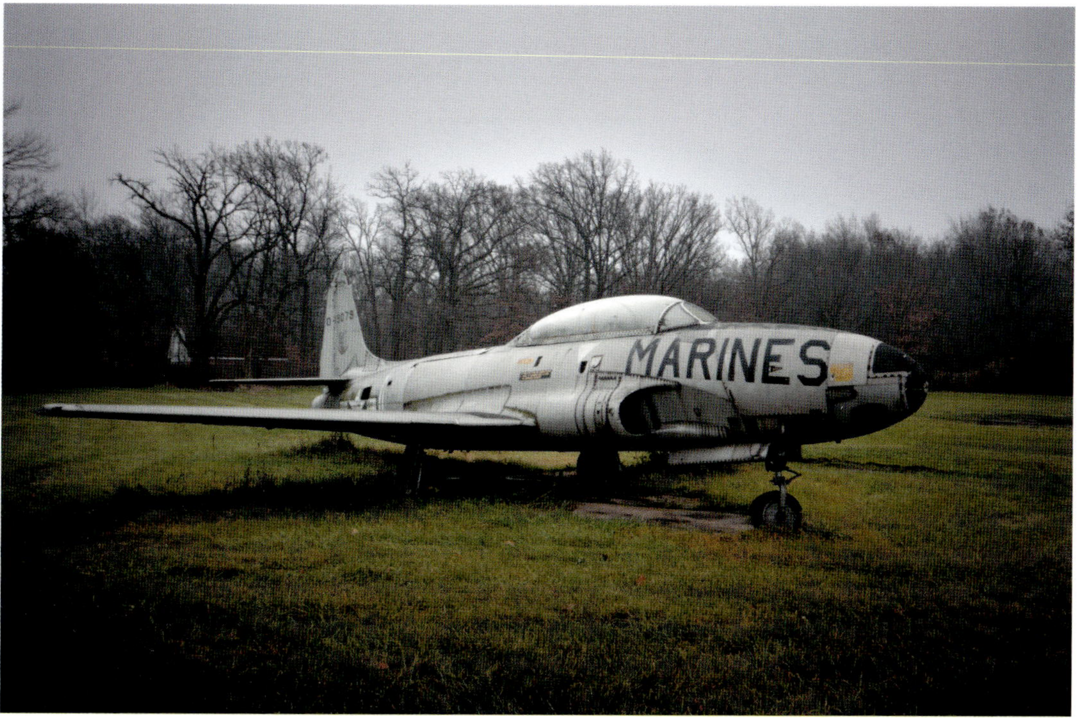

The marine corps jet of general ennui.

9

DREAMS, NIGHTMARES, AND FLIGHTS OF FANCY

People curious about urban exploration frequently want to know if I've experienced something supernatural while shooting, or how creepy abandoned places are in general. As much as I love a good story and hate to disappoint, I personally have never seen a ghost or spirit, or come across anything remotely haunted or that would otherwise make me second guess the laws of physics. The scariest thing an explorer may likely encounter is the police, or perhaps some other disgruntled authority figure. The answer to the second question, however, is a bit more nuanced.

On some level, the places and things pictured in this book reside in a parallel world. They exist divorced from our human scale of time, with its structure and schedules. Unmoored this way, the rot, neglect, vandalism, and theft within begin to change them. Sometimes, the effect is to add a patina of decay to an otherwise recognizable place. Other times, they can seem to become something entirely other. Are they creepy? Perhaps, but a better answer is that they become the stuff of dreams, with their own rules and sensibilities.

At its best, urban exploration takes me into this realm of the other. Fantastic sights lay at the end of the longest hallways or in the dimmest basements, waiting to be discovered. Sometimes, they are seen just by squinting and looking through the ruins, or they could be accidents of lighting in murky interiors. And at other times, they are a fusion of the place with the imagination of the photographer.

It can start simply. Strange perspectives and a jumble of shapes and light can create disorienting vistas in old factory spaces. As a good friend once told me when she got a shot that I had entirely missed, "Always look up."

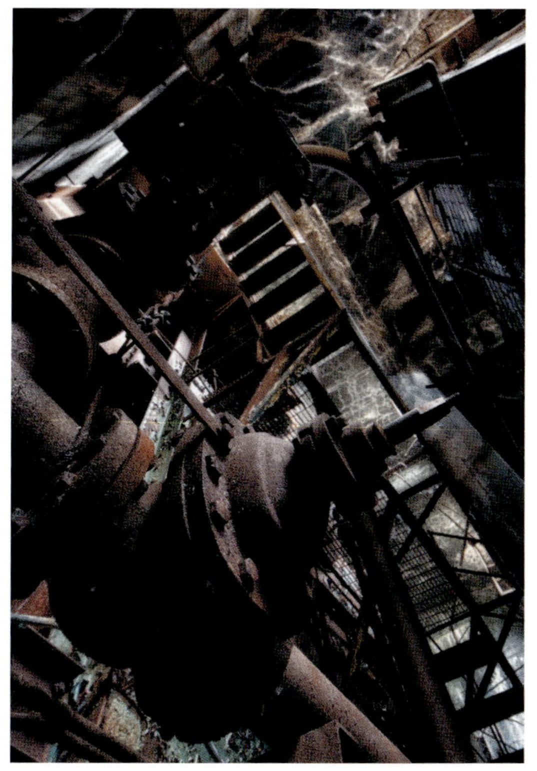

Look up.

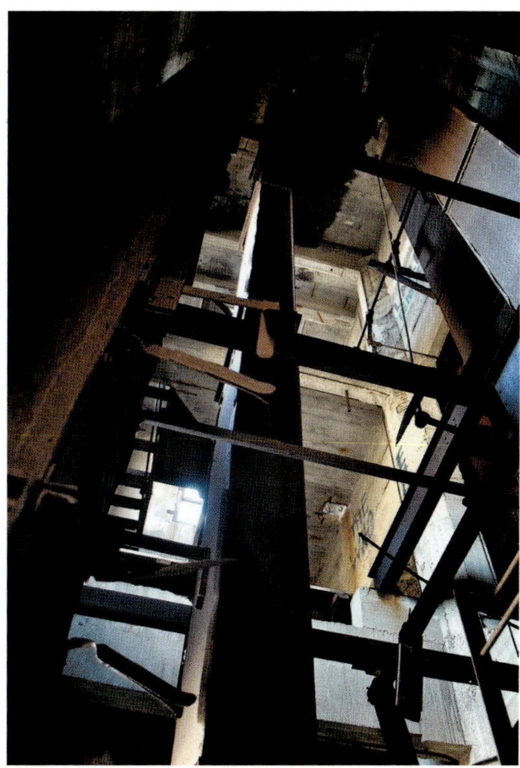

Sentries of the shaft.

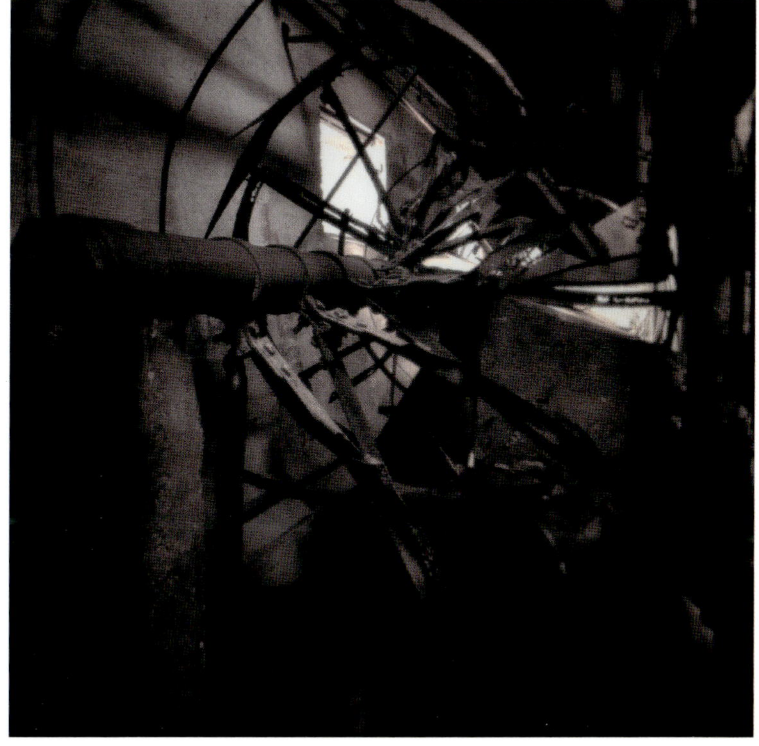

Spiral.

Furniture and equipment may shift or fall as buildings decay, creating chaotic new patterns or revealing previously invisible things. In these cases, drop ceilings eroded away until all their lights came loose and dropped. Standing among these fixtures gave the impression of being caught in a great frozen kinesis, like a frozen meteor shower.

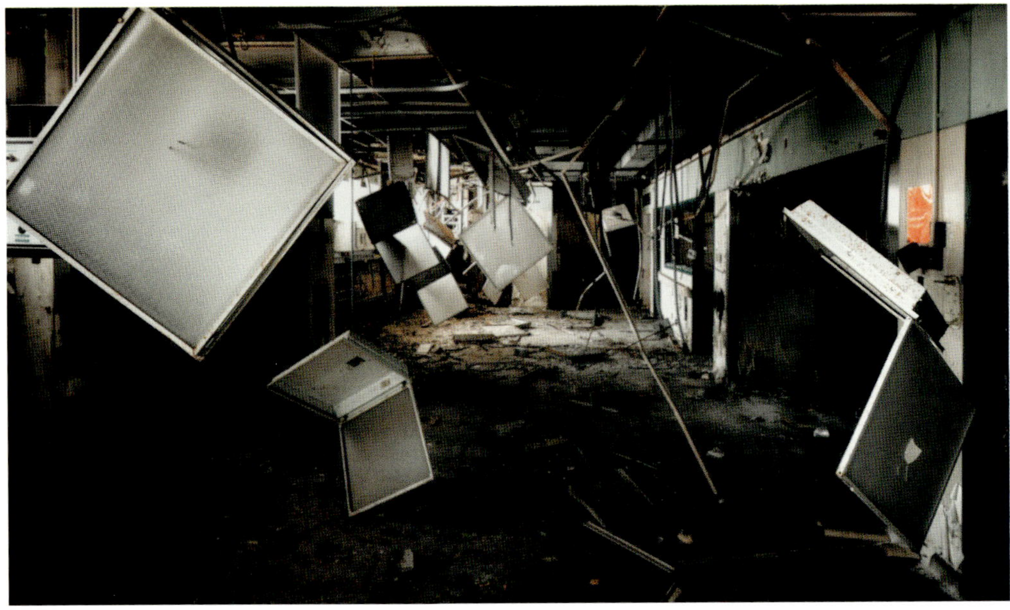

Meteor field 1 (above) and meteor field 2 (below).

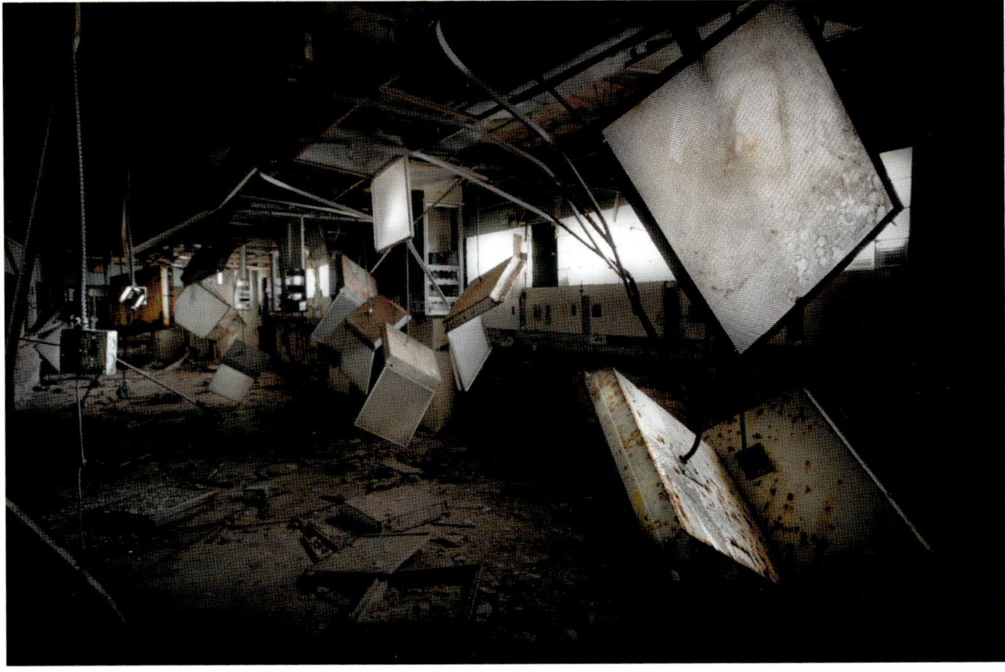

The right light can take an ordinary scene an make it appear otherworldly. A building adjacent to a derelict factory was possibly once used for storage. Its corrugated metal roof has weathered unevenly, and rust has eaten hundreds of small holes through the steel. The result is something that was dubbed the "Disco Room."

Other times, the sun will break through the roof or a window, spilling a beam of light across a dim interior. Depending on the time and place as well as one's demeanor, these shafts of furtive light may be seen as beautiful, menacing, or auspicious, and at times, maybe even creepy.

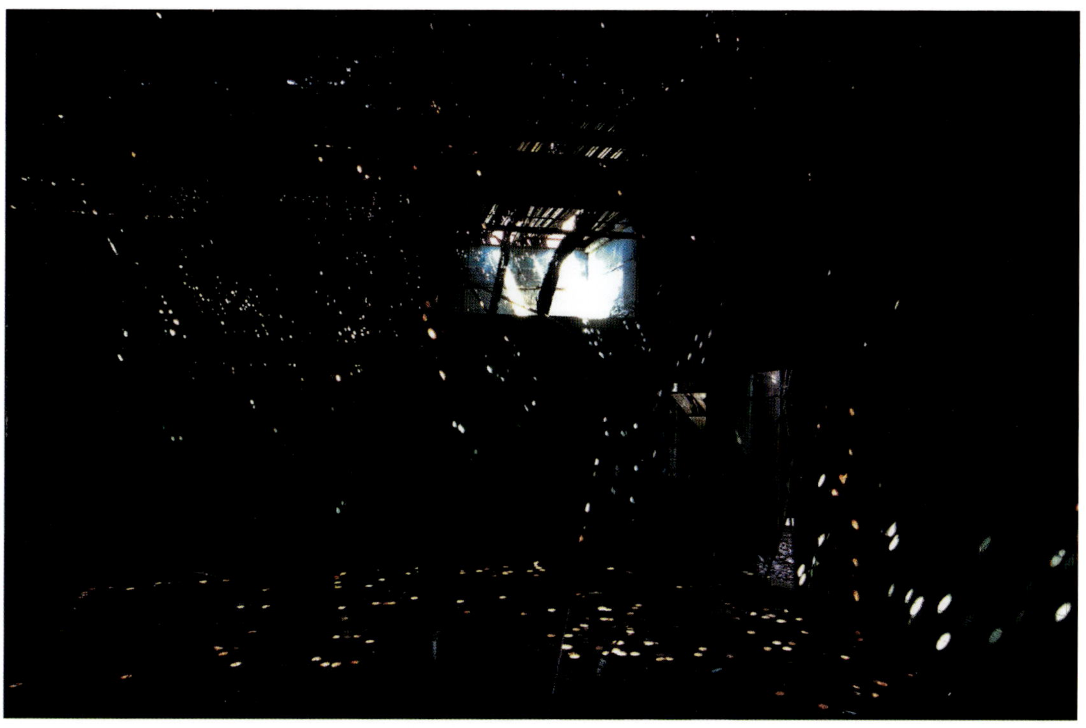

Sometimes, the room seemed filled with starlight.

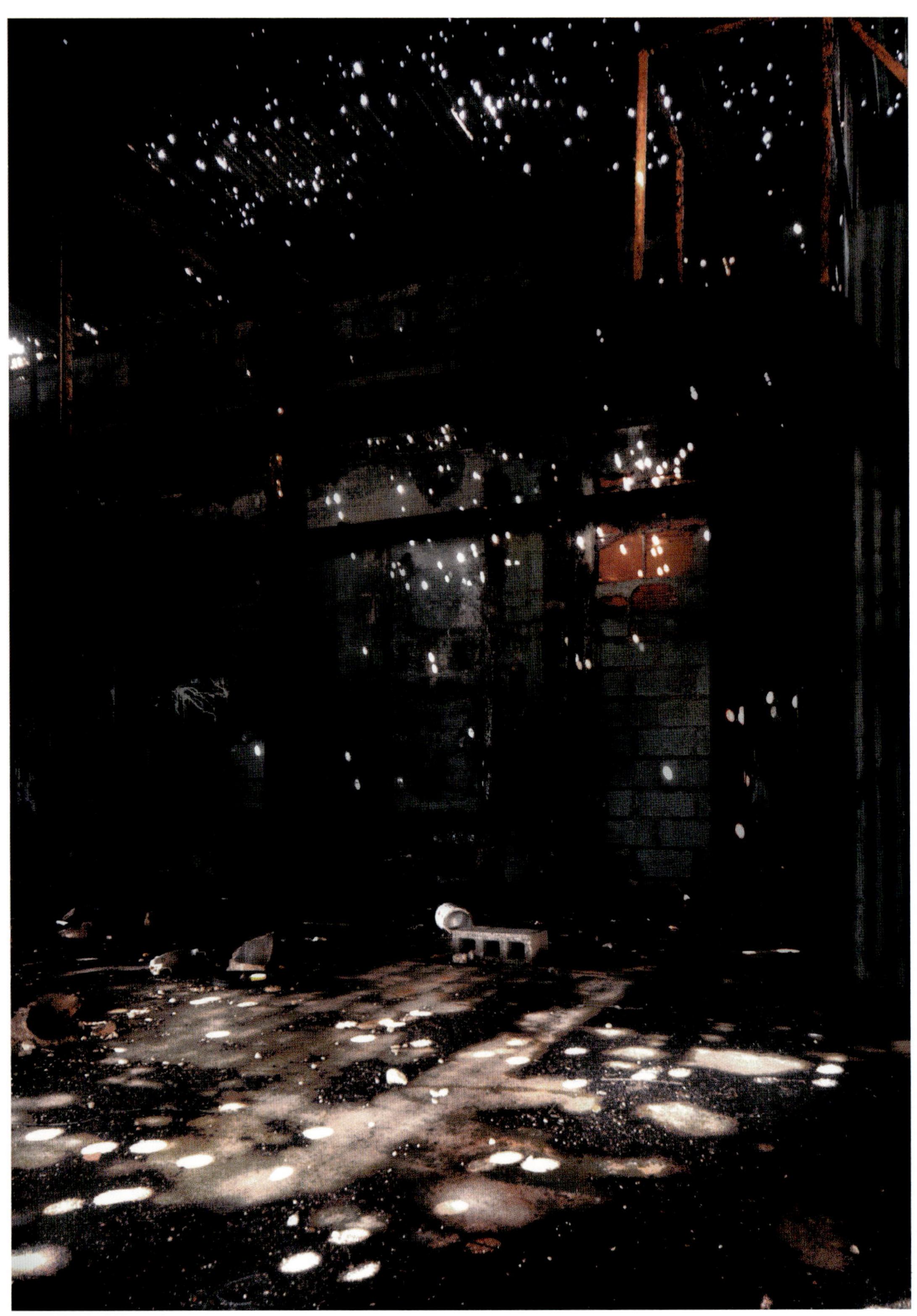

At other times, it resembled a disco floor.

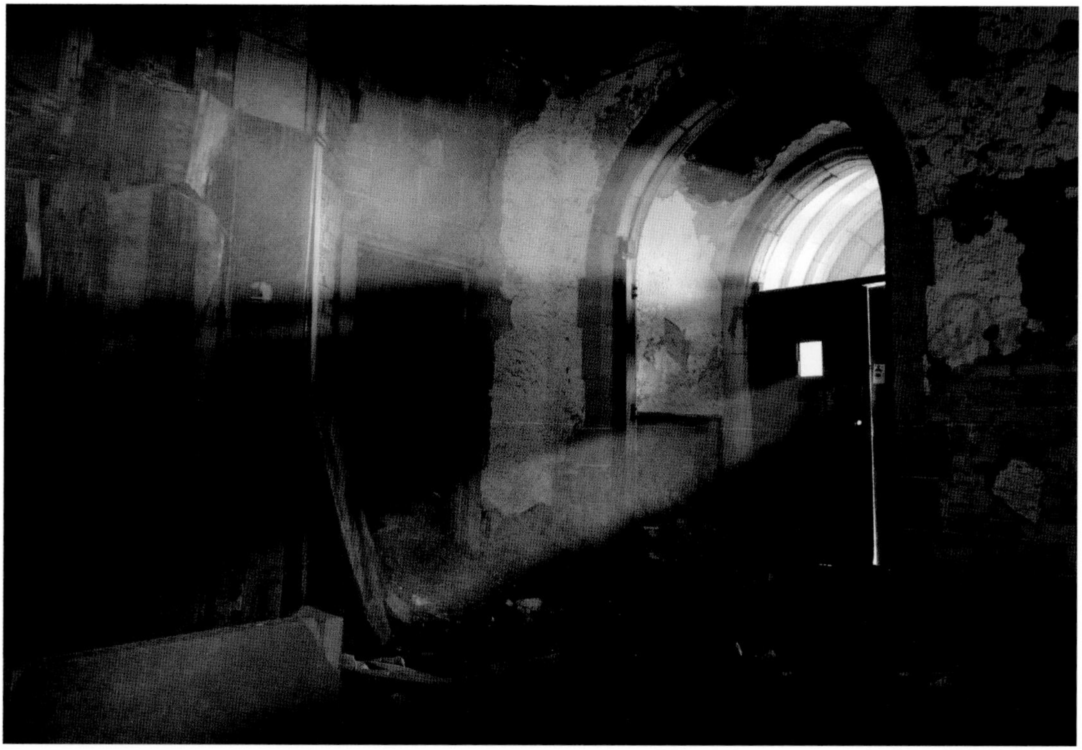

Long summer afternoon light comes through church doors.

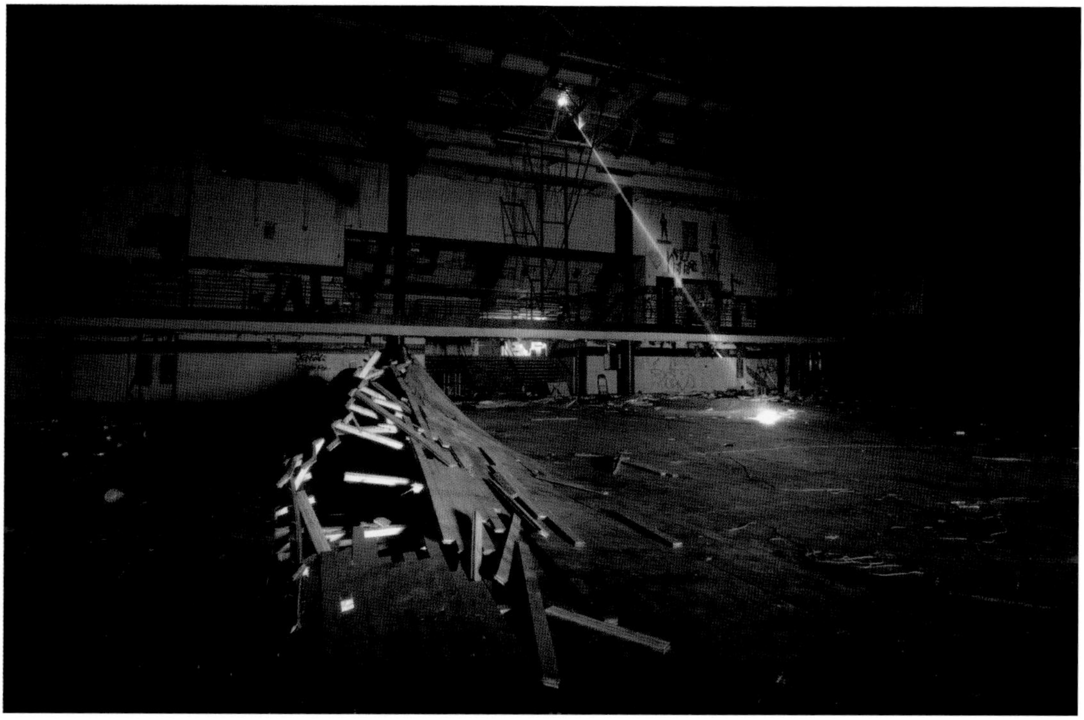

Years of exposure to the elements causes a high school gym floor to tsunami.

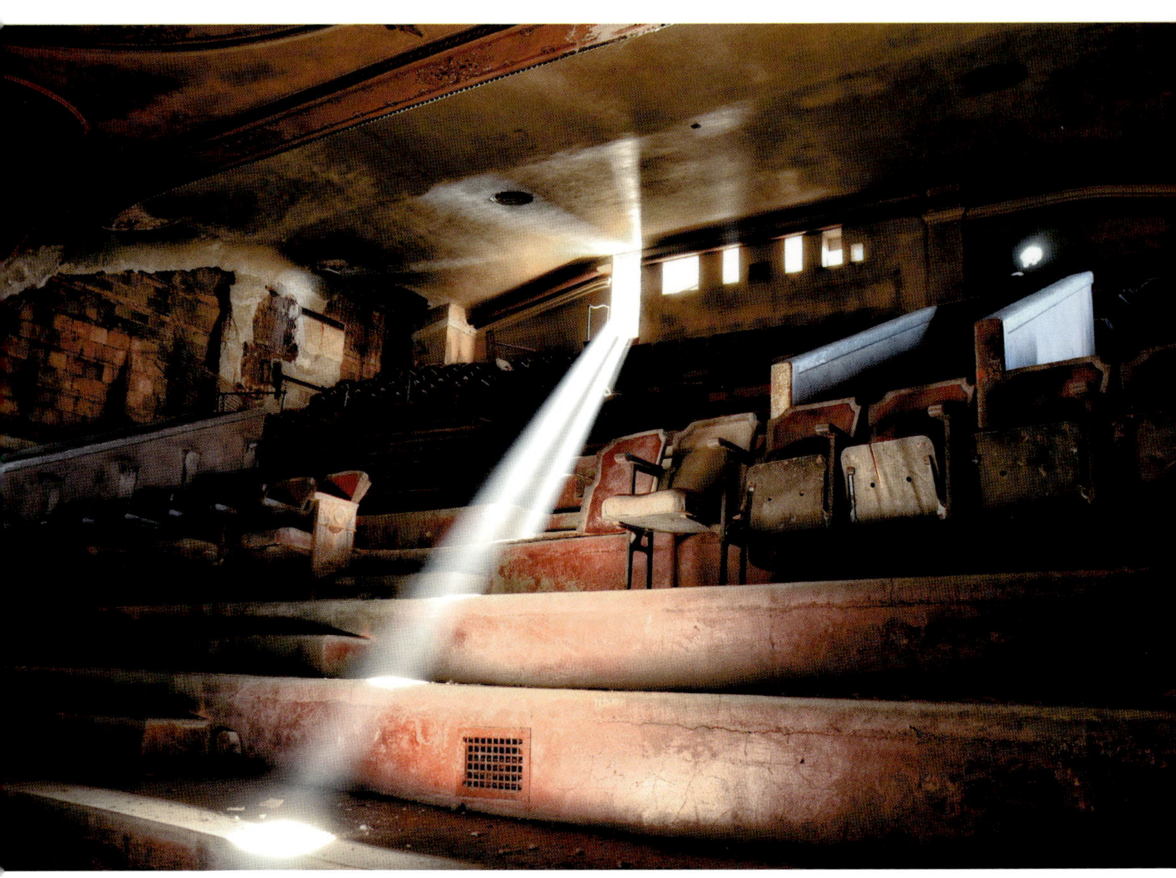

A sunbeam tracks across a theater balcony.

Finally, human actions can evoke singular scenes, usually with paint or light. In the first case, graffiti is something I usually ignore. It can create more color or texture within a particular room, but usually exists only as background noise for me. But the writing on the wall of this hospital room was too perfectly rendered to ignore. Whether created intentionally by a previous photographer, or by some random kid as a prank, it had a nightmarish quality I couldn't ignore.

Lighting a scene in total darkness can be daunting. Using a flash seldom yields good pictures, as the harsh light of a flashbulb usually creates deep shadows and washed out, overly bright areas. The solution is usually light painting. Using flashlights, cell phones or even glow sticks or road flares, a photographer can carefully light different parts of the frame for differing lengths of time, hopefully creating a decent photo without too much glare or obvious shadows. But an explorer's whimsy can take over, and the subject matter can be made to look ethereal, unreal, or even infernal.

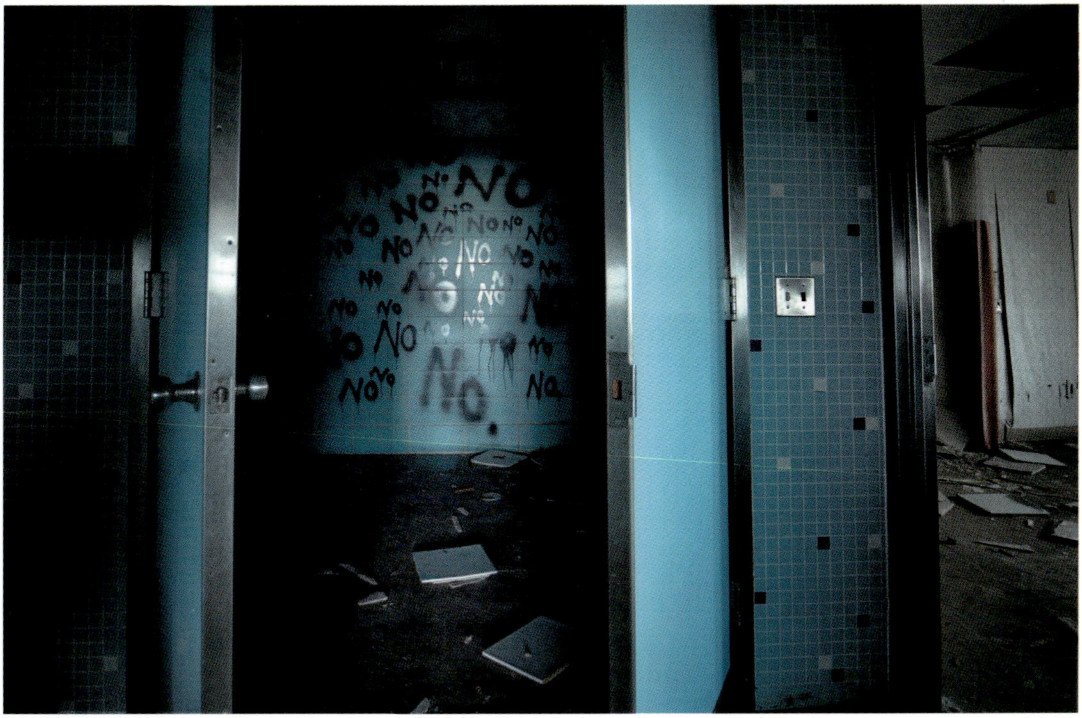

The answer is no.

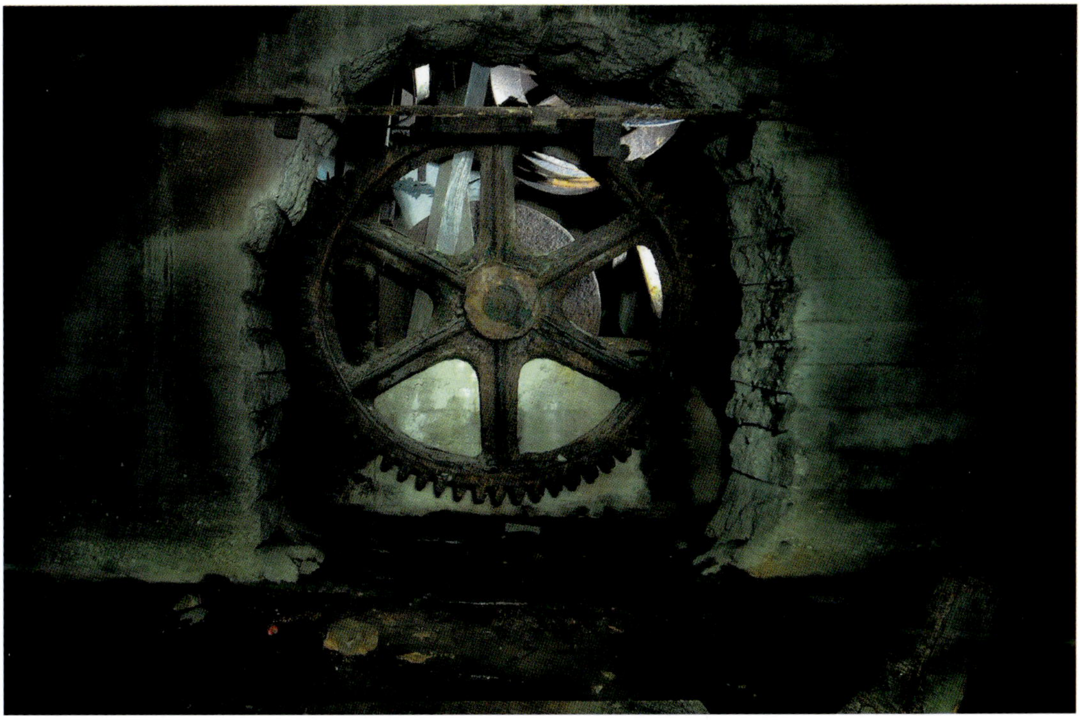

Subterranean gears sit rusted shut below a south side silo complex.

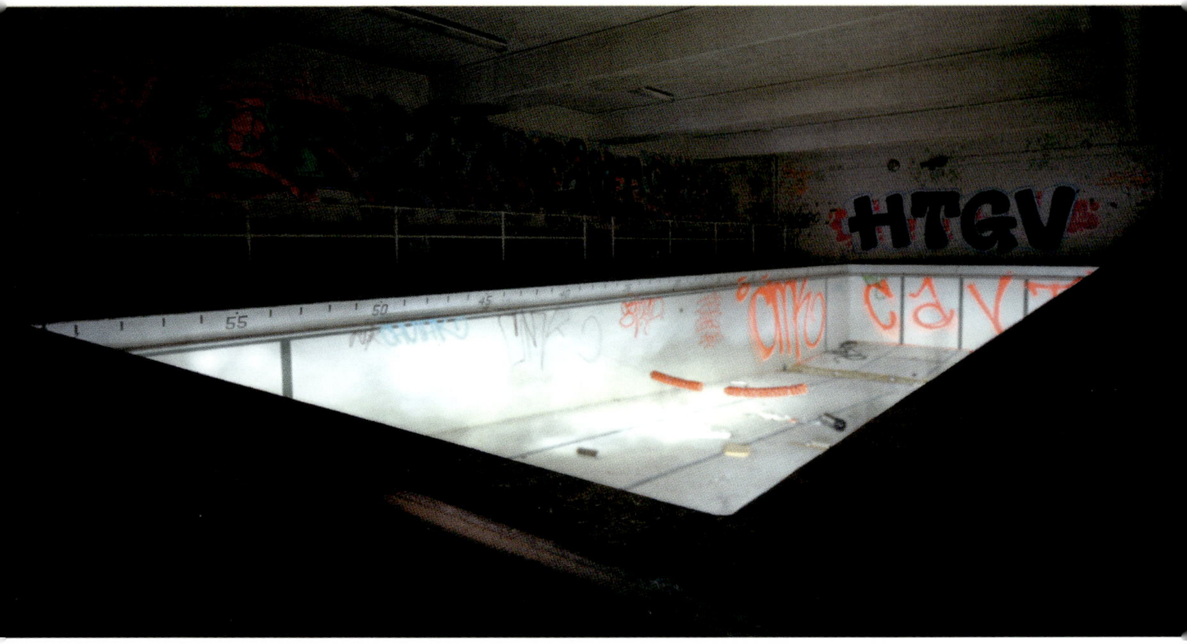

Pool haunted by a photographer with a flashlight.

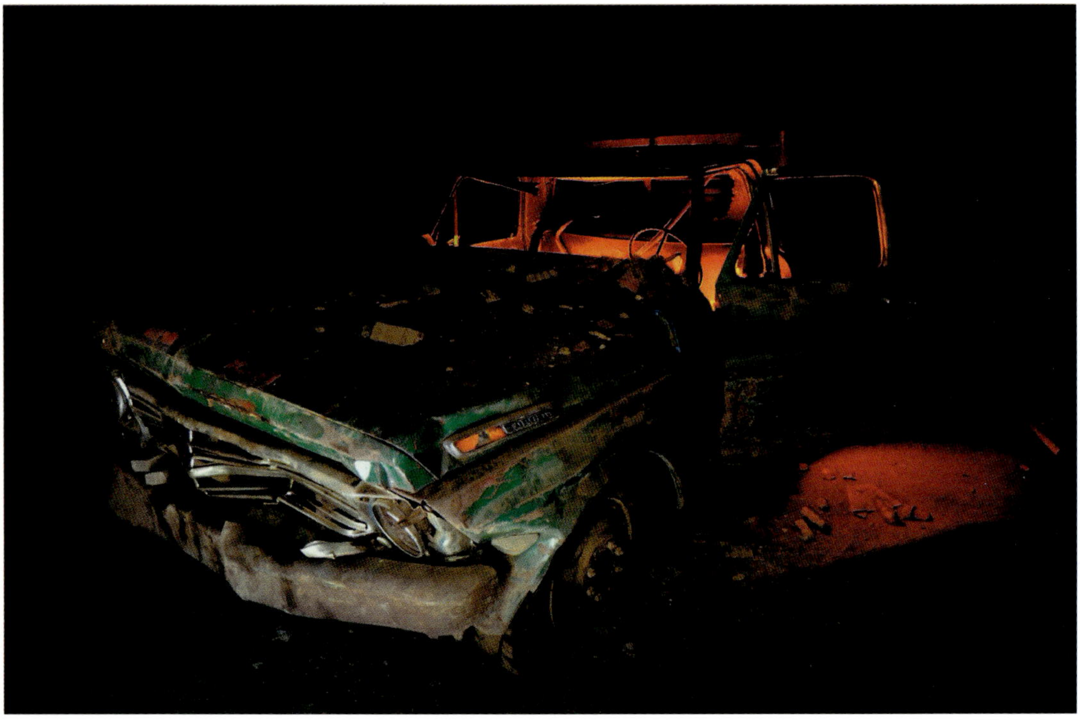

The 1977 Oldsmobile Nightmare d'Elegance is the preferred vehicle of demons and the undead.

10

CODA

As cities grow and change, they leave in their wake abandoned churches and factories, and ruined homes and businesses. And, though it hides the skeletons in its closet better than most, Chicago is no different. This churn of destruction and rebirth may be seen as inevitable, but it has real consequences for people and the places where they once lived, worked, or prayed. We gain nothing if we turn away from the blight or abandonment in our neighborhoods and only celebrate the conventionally pretty parts of our city. In doing so, we may lose some of our history, along with an appreciation of the beauty hidden within it. At times, as much as we want order and affirmation, a *memento mori* is salutary.

> In order for the light to shine so brightly, the darkness must be present.
>
> Francis Bacon

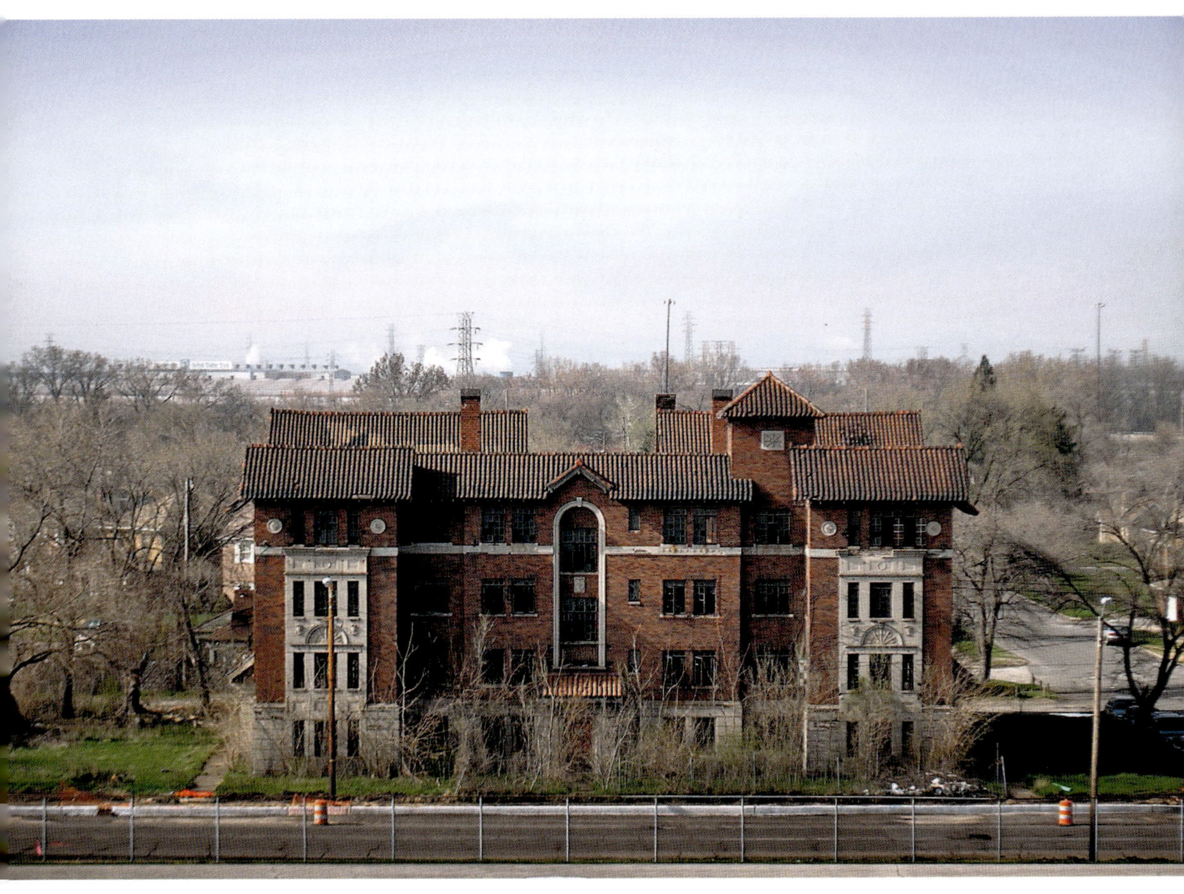

This Gary apartment building was my first ever exploration.